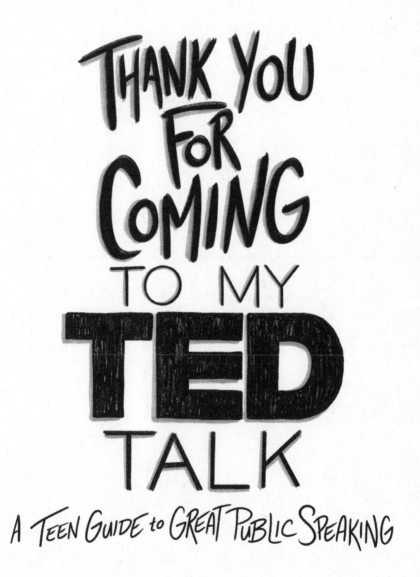

THANK YOU FOR COMING TO MY TED TALK

A Teen Guide to Great Public Speaking

THANK YOU FOR COMING TO MY TED TALK

A Teen Guide to Great Public Speaking

BY CHRIS ANDERSON

with LORIN OBERWEGER

HOUGHTON MIFFLIN HARCOURT
BOSTON   NEW YORK

hmhbooks.com

The text was set in Stempel Garamond LT Std.
Design by Andrea Miller

Library of Congress Cataloging-in-Publication Data

Names: Anderson, Chris, 1957 January 14– author. | Oberweger, Lorin, author. Title: Thank you for coming to my TED talk : a teen guide to great public speaking / by Chris Anderson, with Lorin Oberweger. Other titles: TED talk : a teen guide to great public speaking Description: Boston : Houghton Mifflin Harcourt, 2020. | Includes bibliographical references. | Audience: Ages 10 to 12 | Audience: Grades 5–7 | Summary: "A teen edition of the New York Times best-selling TED TALKS: The Official TED Guide to Public Speaking, chock-full of tips and techniques to help teens become confident, capable speakers" —Provided by publisher. Identifiers: LCCN 2019029204 (print) | LCCN 2019029205 (ebook) ISBN 9781328995070 (hardcover) | ISBN 9780358326625 (ebook) Subjects: LCSH: Public speaking—Handbooks, manuals, etc.—Juvenile literature. Classification: LCC PN4129.15 .A535 2020 (print) | LCC PN4129.15 (ebook) | DDC 808.5/1—dc23
LC record available at https://lccn.loc.gov/2019029204
LC ebook record available at https://lccn.loc.gov/2019029205

Manufactured in the United States of America
DOC 10 9 8 7 6 5 4 3 2 1
4500788789

This book is dedicated
to Zoe Anderson,
whose too-short life
is remembered
at zoecoral.com.

CONTENTS

ONSTAGE

YOUR TURN

INTRODUCTION

BRINGING THE FIRE

The houselights dim. A young girl—her palms sweating, her legs trembling—steps out onto the stage. A spotlight hits her face, and twelve hundred pairs of eyes lock on to hers. The audience senses her nervousness. Tension thickens the air. She clears her throat and starts to speak.

What happens next is astounding.

Twelve hundred brains inside the heads of twelve hundred independent individuals start to behave strangely. They begin to sync. A magic spell woven by the girl washes over each person.

They gasp together. Laugh together. Weep together.

Rich patterns of information inside the girl's brain are somehow copied and transferred to the twelve hundred brains in the audience. These patterns will remain in those minds for the rest of their lives, potentially impacting their behavior years into the future. In the most magical of ways, that girl and those listening to her have formed a bond—a connection born of ideas and empathy.

The girl on the stage is weaving wonder, not witchcraft.

But her skills are as potent as any sorcery.

Now picture this:

You're the one on a TED Talk stage, working to create that magical alchemy.

Or you're simply standing in front of a classroom crammed with other students—some who seem more interested in their cellphones than in your presentation.

Maybe you're anxiously awaiting a college interview.

You could be in a play at school or in a community theater.

You might want to create a vlog, podcast, or your own video channel.

Perhaps you're about to apply for a job or participate in your first debate.

It could be you've taken on a cause that means so much to you that you feel you *have* to share your passion with others. Your public speech might extend to the one person who answers his front door, or it might reach a throng of thousands, maybe hundreds of thousands.

Though the average teen might not give TED Talks every day, understanding how to speak publicly, with confidence and courage, is a skill that will serve you always. In big ways and small, you'll be challenged to create that magical connection with others. Sometimes it will be in an academic setting. Other times it will be out in your community, sharing stories from the heart. Now, more than ever, teen voices are heard; they're respected. And they're vital.

The purpose of this book is to explain how the miracle of powerful public speaking is achieved and to equip you to give it your best shot. But one thing needs emphasizing right at the start: *There is no one way to give a great talk.*

While this book will offer guidance in terms of best practices for organizing your speeches and presenting them to the world—including tips for getting to the heart of the story and battling the beasts of fear and procrastination, please know that there's really no set formula and that the best things you can do are *breathe, play,* and *practice, practice, practice.*

Even if there were some kind of successful formula that could be applied *today,* it might feel stale as old potato chips *tomorrow.* That's because part of the appeal of a great talk is its freshness. We're humans. We don't like the same old, same old. The last thing we want is for everyone to sound the same, to have the same take on a topic, or to come at us with the enthusiasm of a robot.

So don't think of this book as a set of *rules* to be followed obediently. Think of it as a toolbox full of goodies you can dip into as needed. It's the sum of a lot of people's experience, all aimed at making speaking easier and more natural for you, at helping you feel more prepared and confident. Take what you need and chuck the rest, but know that you have within you the ability to be a *great* speaker, even if the idea of public speaking makes you want to jump out of your skin or run for the hills.

Your only real job in giving a talk is to have something valuable to say and to say it authentically, in your own unique way. Believe it or not, you may find it more natural than you think—and even, perhaps, more than a little bit fun.

Among every culture on earth, as language developed, people learned to communicate their hopes, dreams, and stories. And in doing so, the human family was born.

Imagine a typical scene.

It is after nightfall. The campfire is ablaze. A cluster of people gather around it, and the air fills with the energy of anticipation.

The story begins. And as the storyteller speaks, each listener imagines the events being described. That imagination brings with it the same emotions shared by the characters in the story.

From this shared experience, it is a short step to the desire to act together, to embark together on a journey, a battle, a building, a celebration.

The same is true today. Public speaking is the key to unlocking empathy, stirring excitement, passing on knowledge and insights, and promoting a common dream. The spoken word has actually gained new powers—and incredible reach across nations, even across the globe.

Our campfire is now the whole world. Thanks to the internet, a single talk in a single theater can end up being seen by millions of people. So can a single speech given at a rally, or even a cellphone message sent from one teen to others who, with it, receive a lifesaving boost of courage or understanding.

Done right, a talk can electrify a room and transform an audience's worldview.

When we peer into a speaker's eyes, listen to the tone of her voice, sense her vulnerability, her intelligence, her passion, we are tapping into unconscious skills that have been fine-tuned over hundreds of thousands of years. Skills that can galvanize, empower, inspire.

And in some venues, we can even present our stories in ways our ancient ancestors could never have imagined. What would it have meant to record and bring the sounds of stampeding wildebeests to our campfire tales? Or to capture a photo of moonrise in a far-off land?

In some ways, those ancient campfire sessions were meant to draw us together, to create safety and unity by reducing the world to understandable bits. Now our safety and unity derive from our understanding of how big the world is, how full of wonder, and—no matter how different people might be, how strange their customs and beliefs may feel to us—how deeply we're all connected. We can all understand and come together via the power of the ideas we communicate, the stories we tell.

We live in a time when the best way to make an impact may be simply to stand up and say something, because both the words and the passion with which those words are delivered can now spread across the world at warp speed. And those words can be spoken by anyone—old or young or in-between.

～

TED began as an annual event that brought together people in the fields of Technology, Entertainment, and Design (hence the clever name, TED). In recent years, it has expanded to cover any topic of public interest. And it has opened to people of all ages, nationalities, abilities, and perspectives. TED speakers enlighten, persuade, and entertain via the delivery of short, carefully prepared talks. And to our delight, these hugely successful events not only draw people in person from around the world but also have proven a hit online, with billions of views annually.

What's more, young speakers have become an increasingly common and vital part of the TED landscape, whether they're invited onto the official TED stage or participate in programs like TEDxTeen, independently organized events (given with permission from the TED organization) that put teens and their concerns front and center.

We also launched TED-Ed Student Talks, a free program that offers young people exciting opportunities to develop and share their own TED Talks. The program's flexible curriculum supports students in identifying, researching, and ultimately sharing their boldest ideas with the world. The boost to the confidence and self-esteem of kids who make it through to the delivered talk is inspiring to see. We think presentation literacy should be a core part of every school's curriculum, on par with reading and math. It's going to be an important life skill.

From Taylor Wilson, who built a working fusion reactor at the age of fourteen, to sixteen-year-old Jack Andraka, who created an early-detection test for pancreatic cancer; from Tavi Gevinson, who began a wildly popular and unapologetically feminist fashion blog called *Style Rookie,* to Memory Banda, who spoke out against the practice of child marriage: these teen speakers have changed the cultural landscape, sparking interest and spreading their ideas well past their own communities.

And they're not alone. Teen scientists, musicians, culture critics, app developers, inventors, and writers have all taken their turns on a TED or TEDxTeen stage. They've all added their voices to a great worldwide conversation. In doing so, they've given permission to other young people to find their voices, to embrace the causes and ideas that are of importance to them. They've helped others understand that they can step into the conversation at any time and become a real force for good.

TED's amazing speakers—of all ages—have completely changed the way we see the world. From our lucky ringside seats, we have been intrigued and infuriated, informed and inspired. We have also had the chance to ask our speakers directly for their advice on how to prepare and deliver an amazing talk. Thanks to their brilliance, we've gained valuable insights into how they achieved something so extraordinary in a compressed amount of time. I'm delighted to bring some of these lessons to a new, younger audience whose voices are valuable, needed, and already changing the landscape in so many ways.

The campfires of old have spawned a new kind of fire. A fire that spreads from mind to mind, screen to screen: the ignition of ideas whose time has come.

This matters.

Every meaningful moment of progress happened because humans shared ideas with one another and then worked to turn those ideas into reality. Whether it was the first time our ancestors joined forces to take down a woolly mammoth, or

Neil Armstrong's first step onto the moon, or then-fifteen-year-old Malala Yousafzai's speech before the United Nations, opening the door for the protection of girls' education in many countries, people have turned spoken words into astonishing shared achievements.

We need that now more than ever. Not just brilliant ideas but eye-to-eye, mind-to-mind, heart-to-heart connections. That may seem a bit over-the-top when you're just trying to get it together for a presentation in AP History, but the skills transfer; they're vital; and they'll serve you—always.

Are you ready?

Let's go light a fire.

Chris Anderson

FOUNDATION

1

WHAT'S YOUR POINT?

Maybe it's a friend—or a parent or a teacher. Maybe it's your minister, rabbi, or imam. But at least one person in your life is sure to be a Rambler. That's the person who turns a one-sentence story into a three-hour snoozefest. The one who has to hark back to the Mesozoic Era to give you the backstory on what happened *this morning.*

I'm assuming that person is not *you,* but if your friends or classmates fidget when you talk, if their eyes glaze over, or they hold back not-so-subtle yawns and check their cellphones every two seconds, well, this section might be especially relevant!

"It happens way too often: You're sitting there in the audience, listening to someone talk, and you know that there is a great talk in that person; it's just not the talk he's giving." That's TED's Bruno Giussani, a man who cannot stand seeing potentially great speakers blow their opportunity.

The point of a talk is to say something meaningful. But many talks never get there. Words and sentences are spoken, of course. Ideas presented. But they don't add up to much. They don't point the listeners somewhere vital. Instead, they leave the audience disinterested and unmoved, sometimes flat-out confused.

In the first TED I organized, one of the speakers began, "As I was driving down here wondering what to say to you . . ."

There followed an unfocused list of observations. Nothing obnoxious. Nothing particularly hard to understand. But nothing revelatory, either. No *aha* moments. No takeaways. The audience clapped politely. But no one really learned anything. No one was changed by the experience.

It's one thing to underprepare. But to boast that you've underprepared? That tells the audience that their time doesn't matter. That the event doesn't matter.

Of course, no one really has to boast that they're underprepared. That becomes obvious pretty quickly. I'll talk more about preparation later, but the point here is that you owe it to your audience, and yourself, to present your material in a clear, focused manner—and to have a point.

As Bruno Giussani puts it, "When people sit in a room to listen to a speaker, they are offering her something extremely precious: a few minutes of their time and of their attention. Her task is to use that time as well as possible."

Rambling is not an option.

There's a helpful word used to analyze plays, movies, and novels; it applies to talks, too. It is *throughline,* the connecting theme that ties together the ideas you're presenting. An understanding of this concept and the way to apply it to any talk will help you vanquish any possibility of rambling.

Famed acting coach Konstantin Stanislavski also used the term "the spine" to convey this idea. Just as a spine supports the structure of your body, a throughline supports the structure of your presentation. It gives it meaning and focus; it's the metaphorical cord that runs through the entire speech.

This doesn't mean every talk can cover only one topic, tell a single story, or proceed in one direction without diversions. Not at all. It simply means that all the pieces need to connect, and they need to stack together to support the main idea.

Here's the start of a talk thrown together without a throughline. "I want to share with you some experiences I had during my recent trip to Cape Town, and then make a few observations about life on the road . . ."

Compare that with: "On my recent trip to Cape Town, I learned something new about strangers—when you can trust them and when you definitely can't. Let me share with you two very different experiences I had . . ."

The first example promises a collection of tidbits, with no real indication of adding up to something meaningful. The second offers an important idea and promises that evidence will be presented to support that idea. As with puzzle pieces, the individual portions of the speech should snap into place to create an overall picture. And like the image on the front of the puzzle box, we should be given a strong sense of how everything will come together.

A good exercise is to try to state your throughline in no more than fifteen words. And remember, this is more than just the goal of your speech ("I want to inspire my classmates" or "I want to talk about Childish Gambino"). It has to be more focused than that. What is the precise idea you want to build inside your listeners? What is their takeaway? What are you trying to prove?

Try to find something unexpected in your throughline. "The importance of hard work" is expected. "A three-day school week leads to smarter students" is a surprise (one your schoolmates will probably cheer, even if the adults are skeptical). Try to find the unexpected idea, the deeper one. Even if you're assigned a topic you don't love or given a position to debate that's the opposite of your true feelings, try to come at it from a unique angle.

Here are the throughlines of some popular TED Talks, several from teen speakers. Notice that there's an *unexpectedness* incorporated into each of them.

- More choice actually makes us less happy.
- With body language, you can fake it till you become it.
- Adults have much to learn from kids.
- The violin's sixteenth-century "technology" still seems advanced today.
- Online videos can humanize the classroom and revolutionize education.
- My stutter makes me a better public speaker.

Barry Schwartz, whose talk is the first one in the list above, on the paradox of choice, is a big believer in the importance of a throughline:

> The key is to present just one idea—as thoroughly and completely as you can. What is it that you want your audience to [understand completely] after you're done?

Your throughline doesn't have to be as ambitious as the ones listed above. But it still should have some kind of intriguing angle. Instead of giving a talk about the importance of hard work, how about speaking on why hard work sometimes *fails* to achieve true success, and what you can do about that? Instead of some important public figure's whole biography, why not offer a talk about a pivotal time in that figure's life or the way that person revolutionized some specific part of our culture?

Just as it's helpful to state your thesis at the beginning of a paper you write, it can be helpful to offer your throughline as you launch into your talk.

While your speech's spine doesn't always have to be made explicit, you'll find that when your audience knows where you're headed, it's much easier for them to follow. It may also be more engaging for them, because it will build anticipation of the fact that you're going to support the throughline you promise.

FOUNDATION

2

AUDIENCE OF ONE

Best-selling author Elizabeth Gilbert believes in planning a talk for an audience of one.

> Choose a human being—an actual human being in your life—and prepare your talk as if you will be delivering it to that one person only. Choose someone you really like. This will bring a warmth of spirit and heart to your talk. You don't have to go to their house and practice your talk on them for six months; they don't even need to know that you're doing this. Just choose your one ideal listener, and then do your best to create a talk that would blow their mind, or move them, or fascinate them, or delight them.

Most important of all, says Gilbert, is to pick a topic that lives deep within you. "Talk about what you know. Talk about what you know and love with all your heart. I want to hear about the subject that is most important to your life."

Again, as a young speaker, you may not always have control over your choice of topic. But whenever you can, try to find the angle that feels personally compelling to you and to that one audience member whose heart and mind you hope to reach.

—

The goal of one of Elizabeth Gilbert's first TED Talks was to change the way we think about creative genius. Instead of imagining that genius is part of some people's makeup and you either have it or you don't, she wanted the audience to think of it as something that you may *receive* from time to time as a gift, if you make yourself ready for it.

Put just like that, it may not sound very convincing, but Gilbert used her brilliance as a storyteller to persuade us otherwise. She started by being personal, treating the audience like that one special person who could understand her terror at the prospect of having to repeat the success of her bestseller *Eat, Pray, Love* (which was also made into a feature film). She described not only her fear but the "well-intended" concern of those around her who asked, over and over, what it felt like to know her greatest success was behind her.

She then expanded the story beyond herself, sharing hilarious and touching anecdotes of famous creatives who angsted over their inability to perform on demand. What would it do for all artists, she speculated, if they considered how the term *genius* was viewed differently in history, not as something you *were,* but as something that came to you?

Only then could she share a story about the poet Ruth Stone, who told her of the moment when she sensed a poem was coming.

And she felt it coming, because it would shake the earth under her feet. She knew that she had only one thing to do at that point, and that was to, in her words, run like hell. And she would run like hell to the house and she would be getting chased by this poem, and the whole deal was that she had to get to a piece of paper and a pencil fast enough so that when it thundered through her, she could collect it and grab it on the page.

What would have seemed an outlandish story if presented at the start of the talk seemed totally natural by the end. We come to believe not that people *are* geniuses but that they *have* geniuses—not so different from the idea of Muses or other beings bringing us inspiration and the talent to express it.

Sometimes hearts and minds need to be primed a bit—prepared so that the big ideas "stick" better and remain with us longer. In each step of her talk, Gilbert uses her powers of persuasion and her intimate connection with the audience to help us not only accept her main idea but embrace it.

3

TACKLING TOUGH TOPICS

Sometimes, whether in class or perhaps when you're out in the world advocating for some cause, you may be called upon to deal with a heavy subject. It could be a disturbing historical event or a current political or social crisis. It could be something in your own life that's difficult but necessary to discuss. Or it could be the experience of someone else whose plight it's important to share.

Often speakers on these kinds of topics view their job as just bringing these issues into the light. Typically such talks lay out facts to illustrate how awful a situation is and why something must be done to fix it. Indeed, there are times when that is the perfect way to frame a talk—provided you're confident that your listeners are ready and willing to be made to feel uncomfortable.

The trouble is that when audiences sit through too many talks like this, they tend to get emotionally exhausted and start to shut down. Compassion fatigue sets in. It's not uncommon to feel sensitive to—and overwhelmed by—topics that are raw and emotionally troubling.

How can you solve that problem? First, think about your talk as being not about an *issue* but about an *idea*. Multimedia producer June Cohen framed the difference this way:

- An issue-based talk leads with *morality*. An idea-based talk leads with *curiosity*.
- An issue exposes a *problem*. An idea proposes a *solution*.
- An issue says, "Isn't this *terrible?*" An idea says, "Isn't this *interesting?*"

It's much easier to pull in an audience by framing the talk as an attempt to solve a puzzle rather than as a plea for them to care. The first feels like a gift being offered. The second feels like an ask.

Remember your audience of one. It's important to understand that people want to feel included, not accused. Lectures about human wastefulness, with shocking images of sea turtles caught in six-pack rings, can pack a real emotional punch and stir up a lot of guilt, but people will likely feel more moved to action when they hear success stories about conservation efforts and innovations that help preserve the environment.

Hope does more to energize people than despair. Understanding does more than anger. As unjust as the world may seem, we respond not to the idea of what's broken but to the possibility of making things whole.

TALK TOOLS

4

THE JOURNEY

There's one other beautiful metaphor for a great talk. It is a *journey* that speaker and audience take together. Speaker Tierney Thys puts it this way:

> Like all good movies or books, a great talk is transporting. We love to go on adventures, travel someplace new with an informed, if not quirky, guide who can introduce us to things we never knew existed, incite us to crawl out windows into strange worlds, outfit us with new lenses to see the ordinary in an extraordinary way . . . enrapture us and engage multiple parts of our brains simultaneously. So I often try to fashion my talks around embarking on a journey.

If you, the speaker, want the audience to come with you, you probably need to give them a hint of where you're going. And then you need to be sure that each step of the journey helps get you there.

In this journey metaphor, *the throughline traces the path that the journey takes.* It ensures that there are no impossible leaps, and that by the end of the talk, the speaker and audience have arrived at their destination together.

The journey on which you take your audience might be one of **exploration**, **explanation**, **persuasion**, or **revelation**. Or, of course, it might include elements of two or more of these concepts.

An **exploratory** talk invites the audience to dive deeply into a topic, to experience some part of the world, some person or creature in a way that invites questions and sparks wonder. It may lead the viewer to some conclusions, but not before lighting up their synapses through the simple act of taking them along into unexplored (or underexplored) realms.

Think of an exploratory talk as an expedition, led by an enthusiastic and knowledgeable guide. The best presenter will work hard to engage all of her audience's senses—giving us much to do with our eyes and ears, even helping us imagine smells and tactile sensations.

The idea of exploration conveys substance. We're not given lots of tidbits about a number of things. It's not a survey but a study—the difference between visiting ten countries in ten days and settling into one city in order to really understand what it's like to live there, experiencing as many of its treasures as possible. An exploration leaves us with a rich understanding and a feeling of time well spent.

A journey of **explanation** is, well, pretty self-explanatory. It's a talk that seeks to convey knowledge to the audience, clarifying a topic or taking the viewer through a particular procedure.

One great, albeit brief, example came from TED speaker and young inventor William Kamkwamba, whose construction of a windmill changed the lives of his family, his community in Malawi, and certainly himself.

Our exchange on the TED stage took the audience through an explanation of the windmill's creation, the reasoning for its four-blade design, and how it was initially put to use.

> **William Kamkwamba:** I made four blades, just because I want to increase power.
>
> **Chris Anderson:** And what did you make the windmill out of? What materials did you use?
>
> **WK:** I use a bicycle frame, and a pulley, and plastic pipe, what then pulls—
>
> **CA:** And so, and that windmill, what—it worked?
>
> **WK:** When the wind blows, it rotates and generates.
>
> **CA:** How much electricity?
>
> **WK:** Twelve watts.
>
> **CA:** And so that lit a light for the house? How many lights?
>
> **WK:** Four bulbs and two radios.

What's vital to note about an explanation-based talk is that the explanation gains power and interest through *context*. The audience felt riveted by my conversation with William because of the life-changing circumstances involved in the creation of that windmill. If I'd been onstage with the president of an energy company, with all the knowledge and resources she might be expected to have, the explanation of the windmill's creation would be far less interesting.

So always remember the emotional underpinnings of any kind of talk. An explanation is given power by the audience's desire for that explanation. If they're not likely to feel intense interest in your topic or circumstances, you might want to reframe the kind of talk you give.

—

The **persuasive** journey: Another form of talk is one that seeks to persuade the audience of something vital. For example, it may ask the audience to accept a certain idea or might work to move them to a certain course of action.

Let's go back to the idea of a talk as a journey you take your audience on. You may have figured out a brilliant route to a powerful destination. But before you can take people there, you have to make the journey seem enticing. For this, we rely on the power of persuasion.

Artist Shantell Martin, for example, wanted to persuade her TEDxTeen audience that *everyone* is capable of drawing, of finding a form of art that speaks to them.

And activist Sophie Umazi thought she could use the power of photography to help prevent future violence between different tribes in her beloved home of Kenya. When people all over her country took photographs of themselves with the label I AM KENYAN, they opened the door to recognition of their similarities rather than fear of their differences. Her TEDxTeen talk aims to persuade audiences of the same idea—that the power of photography can not only change lives but also bring peace to places that have been formerly troubled with violence.

It's important to note that knowledge can't be *pushed* into a brain. It has to be *pulled* in. In other words, persuasion doesn't generally come via shouting or even lecturing. Before you can build an idea in someone else's mind, you need their permission. You can give the most brilliant talk, but if you don't first connect with the audience, it just won't land.

Your first job as a speaker, then, is to build a trusting human bond with the audience so that they're willing—delighted, even—to offer you full access to their minds for a few minutes. Persuasive talks often gently coax viewers from their place of certainty—of feeling they know things "for sure"—to a new way of looking at those very ideas. It may take photographic or video proof to do your persuading. Or it might be as simple as telling a story from your life, asking your audience questions, and leading them to unexpected answers. Whatever methods you use, the best persuasive talks put the speaker on the side of the audience first and then invite the audience to come over to the speaker's side.

Finally, a **revelatory** talk obviously seeks to *reveal* something to the audience. But that revelation should have some surprise element, some compelling hook that makes the audience come alive, experience an idea in a new way.

And what's the most direct way of gifting an idea to an audience?

Simply by *showing* it to them.

Many talks are anchored this way. You reveal your work to the audience in a way that delights and inspires.

You might show a series of images from a new art project and talk through it. Or you might give a demonstration of something you've invented or of a scientific theory being put to work (think school-science-project displays). You might reveal some important truth via a spoken-word piece or a sermon in your place of worship.

Here, the idea of revelation is not only about demonstrating an idea or taking the viewer on a particular journey. That's part of it. But a revelatory talk pulls back the curtain in some way—often simply by revealing something at the heart of the speaker's personal experiences. It might shock or startle the audience, but in a way that is profound and impactful, not just for the sake of being shocking.

Revelation talks come in an infinite variety, and their success depends on what is being revealed.

In a talk based on images, your main goal might just be to create a sense of wonder and aesthetic delight. If it's a demo, you're probably seeking to amaze and to create a new sense of possibility. If it's a vision of the future, you want it to be so vivid and compelling that your audience makes it their own. And if it's a talk based on your experiences and some surprising conclusion you are inviting the viewer to share, you want to leave the audience with some truth they can take into their own hearts and minds.

When I use the idea of a journey as a way to understand effective speaking, I'm appointing you as the leader of the expedition, the one who will guide your audience to someplace meaningful and new, who will consider what you want your audience to come away with, what gift you want them to receive at the end of the road. Whichever metaphor or guiding principle you use, focusing on what you will *give* to your audience is the perfect foundation for preparing your talk.

5

FIND THE STORY

Whether you're working on a class presentation, a dramatic monologue, or simply sharing your own experiences with others, just about every speech begins with story. (I say "just about" because it's possible you might be called upon to conjugate French verbs or recite *pi* to the billionth decimal. In which case, best of luck!)

Stories make us who we are. I mean this literally. The best evidence from archaeology and anthropology suggests that the human mind coevolved with storytelling. That means our brains grew and added complex structures as our practice of creating stories emerged.

Throughout early history, stories brought social status to great storytellers and actionable insights to great listeners. (For example, an attentive listener could learn how to avoid the life-threatening dangers described in a story.) Therefore, those narrating and listening skills became crucial to human development—to our very survival.

On a primitive level, we vibrate to the frequency of story. It's our cellular language. So it's not just that we all love hearing stories. They probably helped shape how our minds share and receive information, how we survive and thrive in our world.

Certainly, the power of stories is evident in today's culture, with streaming services adding story after story, films, limited series, and more. Publishing houses produce tens of thousands of novels and memoirs each year. Movie and TV studios are scrambling for content to feed our love of narrative. And companies like Apple and Google are working to get in on the action too.

Given all of that, it's no surprise that the best talks are anchored in storytelling. Everyone can relate to stories. They typically have a simple linear structure that makes them easy to follow. You just let the speaker take you on a journey, one step at a time. Thanks to our long history around campfires, our minds are great at following along.

A natural part of listening to stories is that you empathize with the experiences of the characters. You find yourself immersed in their thoughts and emotions. In fact, you physically feel what they feel; if they're stressed or excited or exhilarated, so are you.

It's said that our brains can't really distinguish between an experience being told to us (or a story we're reading) and one we're experiencing for real. A good story strikes us in our bodies, makes our hearts race, makes us tingle with excitement or dread. It involves us in a truly physical, meaningful way. Your attention is held. And that makes you care about the outcome.

What are the elements of a great story?

The classic formula is a **protagonist** with **goals** meets an unexpected **obstacle**, usually in the form of a **physical barrier** or **another person** with an **opposing agenda**. Sometimes the obstacle comes from **society**. Sometimes from the **protagonist him- or herself**. The protagonist attempts to **overcome the obstacle**, leading to a **struggle** and the story's **climax**, and finally to a **resolution** in which the goal is **achieved** or **lost**.

Usually there's something in the form of an **inciting incident**—the moment that kicks off the chain of events. And there are other elements as well—plot twists, secondary but important characters, sacrifices, and so on. But figuring out what your speech's subject sought, why he sought it, and why this particular pursuit meant something can give your talk both necessary shape and, more important, meaning.

Let's look at an example of someone I mentioned earlier—Malala Yousafzai. If you were putting together a speech about her, you might begin with the moment that set things into motion for her—when men climbed aboard her school bus and shot her, point blank, simply because she was a girl who wanted an education and worked to encourage the education of other girls in her region of Pakistan.

That moment led to her leaving Pakistan for medical treatment, which also began her crusade to spread the cause of girls' education around the globe. The pursuit of that goal, perhaps culminating in her amazing speech before the United Nations, might make up the body of your talk.

Another helpful way to pull together the most gripping parts of the story for your speech is to remember the acronym **SWAG**, which stands for **Stakes, World, Action,** and **Goals**.

Let's break those down a bit:

Stakes: Consider what was on the line for the subject of your speech in pursuing the goal driving them on their journey. What stood to be lost if they didn't achieve their desired aim? What stood to be gained? In other words, why does this person's journey *matter*? How does it relate to who we are today?

If you were speaking about the life of Annie Sullivan, for example, you might consider that what was at stake for her young student Helen Keller was the whole world. If Sullivan had been unable to break through to Helen, to help her learn to communicate with—and relate to—those around her, the girl would have remained angry and painfully isolated, possibly for the entirety of her life. In a very real way, the stakes could be considered life and death.

World: This gives critical context for your story. It helps frame for the listener the cultural or political structures, even the physical elements that play into your subject's quest. Sometimes the world in your presentation might be a real, concrete location. Sometimes, however, the world could be the world of some profession; that of some art form or sport; a tribe; maybe even the world populated by you and your friends.

Many times, the world around a person shapes who they become or provides obstacles to their becoming what they desire. The world in which Malala Yousafzai sought knowledge, for example, was so hostile to the simple idea of girls' education that an attempt was made on her life. Helping your audience understand the world that serves as a backdrop to your subject's struggle can add dimension to your speech, inviting your listener on a journey through space and time.

Sometimes the world itself might play the major role in your speech. If you're talking about a mission to Everest or Mars or even to the bottom of the sea, that unique environment is sure to fire the listener's imagination. With mere words—and perhaps images as well (which we'll get to later)—you're carrying your audience across the globe, perhaps across the solar system. Who wouldn't be fascinated by that?

Action: The story of someone who is merely a victim of intolerance, injustice, or harm may certainly draw your audience's sympathy. Almost any caring person will feel for the downtrodden or mistreated. However, a story about someone who *acts* to right injustice, to fight against the forces oppressing her, to rally back from bodily injury, unjust treatment, or real tragedy is likely to be the subject of a livelier presentation.

That person's actions do not have to be big and showy. Heroes don't have to wrestle bears or pole-vault over volcanoes. But they do have to *act* in some way to improve their own circumstances and, even better, to improve the circumstances of those around them, possibly even of generations to come.

Someone like Alexander Hamilton (subject of a little Broadway show you might have heard of) committed some bold physical actions, for sure. He made a treacherous voyage from the West Indies to America at the age of seventeen. He fought in the American Revolution. And, unfortunately, he was on the losing end of a famous duel. But what we really remember Hamilton for—at least now, thanks to Lin-Manuel Miranda—is his fervor for helping to grow our nation, to shape many of the institutions that survive to this day. His most significant contributions came from his wit and intellect, not from flashy physical displays.

So your subject's actions don't have to be high-octane feats of physical strength. They can be small and thoughtful but add up to something important, something that creates change in a way that's worth sharing with others.

Goals: As mentioned earlier, a story almost always boils down to a person in pursuit of something important (a goal) meeting obstacles to the attaining of that thing. All of the above items—stakes, world, action—help give context to that pursuit, help us understand the *how* of it, but the driving force of it all is the goal itself.

What's the prize? Where's the finish line?

It might be to land on the moon or to rescue a kitten from a burning building. Or it might be something subtler and more emotional—learning to love yourself, for example, or to understand someone with very different views from your own.

Just as it's helpful to identify these elements in the lives of famous historical figures you might be asked to speak about, it's useful to do this for your own life if you're the subject of your talk. Yes, sometimes you might be asked to give a simple autobiography, but at other times you might be asked to go deeper—to look at your family history, perhaps, and find connected ideas there, or to talk about something that stirs a passion in you—a hobby or social cause, perhaps a book or film or record.

Understanding the SWAG elements, knowing how to shape a story, will help you present yourself—your life and the things that are most important to you—in the most compelling way possible. This is true for book reports, college interviews, debate-team competitions, and so many other arenas in which you'll be asked to speak convincingly—about others *and* about yourself.

A great speech will keep your audience spellbound, anticipating, rooting for the subject to achieve their desired end. We'll do so because we understand the goal and we also understand its significance.

The best talk weaves a powerful tale and takes listeners on an amazing journey. It ends with some feeling of satisfaction, or at least completion. Put a little SWAG in your speech, and the results are bound to be great.

6

TELLING OUR TRUTHS

Often, with stories from our own lives, we overstuff with details that are important to us but that a wider audience just doesn't need to know. Or, worse, we forget an essential piece of context, without which the story doesn't make much sense.

Here's a great story:

Once, when I was eight years old, my father took me fishing. We were in a tiny boat, five miles from shore, when a massive storm blew in. Dad put a life jacket on me and whispered in my ear, "Do you trust me, son?"

I nodded.

He threw me overboard.

I kid you not. Just tossed me over! I hit the water and bobbed up to the surface, gasping for breath. It was shockingly cold. The waves were terrifying. Monstrous.

Then Dad dived in after me. We watched in horror as our little boat flipped and sank. But he was holding me the whole time, telling me it was going to be okay. Fifteen minutes later, the Coast Guard helicopter arrived.

It turned out that Dad knew the boat was damaged and was going to sink. He'd called for help with our exact location.

He guessed it was better to chuck me in the open sea than risk getting trapped when the boat flipped.

And that is how I learned the true meaning of the word *trust*.

⸺

And here's how *not* to tell it:

I learned trust from my father when I was eight years old and we got caught in a storm while out fishing for mackerel. We failed to catch a single one before the storm hit. Dad knew the boat was going to sink, because it was one of those Saturn-brand inflatable boats, which are usually pretty strong, but this one had been punctured once, and Dad thought it might happen again.

In any case, the storm was too big for an inflatable boat, and it was already leaking. So he called the Coast Guard rescue service, who, back then, were available 24/7, unlike today. He told them our location, and then, to avoid the risk of getting trapped underwater, he put a life jacket on me and threw me overboard before jumping in himself.

We then waited for the Coast Guard to come and, sure enough, fifteen minutes later, the helicopter showed up—I think it was a Sikorsky MH-60 Jayhawk—and we were fine.

⸺

Can you feel the difference there? The first story has a character you care about and drama that builds in an unexpected way before being resolved. The second version is a mess. The drama is killed by revealing the father's intent too early; there's no attempt to share the actual experience of the kid; there are too many details included that are irrelevant to most of the audience, while other germane details like the giant waves are ignored. Worst of all, the key line that anchors the story, "Do you trust me, son?" is lost.

If you're going to tell a story about your own life, make sure you know *why* you're telling it, and try to edit out all the details that are not needed to make your point while still leaving enough in for people to vividly imagine what happened.

In seventeen-year-old Natalie Warne's TEDxTeen talk about how anyone has the capacity to change the world, she begins with poignant personal details that effectively tie into the main point of her talk.

> In our small two-bedroom apartment on the South Side of Chicago . . . two pictures hung proudly—one larger-than-life photo of my siblings and me and the other a picture of my mom at twelve years old, staring into the eyes of Dr. Martin Luther King Jr.
>
> When I was younger, I used to stand on my tippy-toes, stare at that picture, close my eyes tightly, and just pretend that it was me gazing up at the man . . . who transformed a generation by his words "I have a dream."

That girl's longing to connect to this towering hero of social justice tells us so much about her values, inviting us not just into her world as a child but into a world where positive change really is possible.

Some of the greatest talks are built around a single personal story. This structure offers huge benefits:

- There's little need for research (it's your life, after all).
- Personal stories, told compellingly, tend to evoke strong audience response.
- You will create empathy for, and interest in, the things you care about most.
- It's easy to remember what you're going to say because the structure is linear, and your brain is extremely comfortable recalling one event right after another.

That said, it's important to remember that the purpose of public speaking is to share, to *give* something to your audience. While it's comforting to speak of yourself because you know your own story, your ultimate goal is to gift the audience with a vital takeaway.

So it's not enough to talk just about your struggles; you also need to talk about what you've *learned* from your struggles, and what *your audience* can learn from your struggles as well. It's important to talk not only about your life experiences but also about the things that have given your life *meaning*, woken you up to some purpose you want to pursue and invite others to pursue as well.

Think about Robert Irwin, the son of Steve Irwin, the television personality and animal conservationist known as the Crocodile Hunter. His father died tragically when Robert was only three years old, and the story he might tell could be of that loss or what it means to live in the shadow of such a famous figure.

But Robert's experiences sparked a passion in him for animal conservation. He felt moved to pursue animal photography, something his father loved, but also to take the Irwin family message to television and books, to give talks around the world, even to bring exotic animals to late-night TV so that global audiences could marvel at the natural world that gives Robert's life purpose.

The bottom line is that we all have experiences worth sharing, but what makes them worth sharing with larger audiences is the meaning we draw from those experiences and impart to others.

Our life stories may entertain or intrigue or make us sound great in the telling. But they don't automatically give the audience something to walk away with: insights, actionable information, context, *hope.*

And that's a real shame. Often, we turn down speakers for TED because while they have interesting lives and tell compelling anecdotes, they're lacking some central idea that wraps the narrative together and gives it meaning outside of their own lives. This is heartbreaking, because frequently the speakers are wonderful, fascinating people. But without the wraparound of an idea and a purpose, it's an opportunity missed.

What's key is to consider the critical moments in your life that offer not just information but *meaning.* If your journey reveals something powerful you've learned or leads to a passion awakened in you that you hope to awaken in us, that's wonderful. If each step in your journey is revealed with humility and honesty and vulnerability, it is a journey we will gladly make with you.

There's one other essential if you're to tell your own story. *It has to be true.* This may seem obvious, but sometimes speakers are tempted to exaggerate or even fabricate. Precisely because a story can have so much impact, they want to cast themselves in the best possible light, and they sometimes cross that line called *truth.*

Don't do that. Remember that your authentic, true self is the greatest gift you can give to an audience. There's no need to embellish your story or fudge the details. Doing so is going to feel cruddy, for one thing, but in this day and age, it's so easy to be caught in a lie. It takes only one person to notice that something's not quite right, and you can find yourself in hot water. It's not worth the risk.

When you combine a truthful story with a desire to help others, you give your listeners an extraordinary gift. Psychologist Eleanor Longden was willing to share publicly how as a young woman she began hearing voices in her head and how that led to her being diagnosed with schizophrenia, institutionalized, and driven to the point of suicide.

The story alone is riveting, but she builds it so that you leave the talk with inspiring insights on schizophrenia, mental illness, and how we might rethink our responses to them.

Here's part of the ending:

There is no greater honor or privilege than facilitating that process of healing for someone; to bear witness, to reach out a hand, to share the burden of someone's suffering, and to hold the hope for their recovery. And likewise, for survivors of distress and adversity, that we don't have to live our lives forever defined by the damaging things that have happened to us. We are unique. We are irreplaceable. What lies within us can never be truly colonized, contorted, or taken away. The light never goes out.

Writer Andrew Solomon described how he was humiliated as a child, and turned the story into an exhilarating essay on identity that anyone could relate to and learn from.

Explorer Ben Saunders went on a trek to the South Pole that almost took his life. He's a powerful storyteller and has great photographs to illustrate what happened. As he drew near the end of his talk, we waited expectantly for the usual prompts to the audience to go out and discover our true selves in whatever challenge we take on.

But Ben surprised us. He shared some dark moments he'd experienced since the trek and said the destination he'd been dreaming of for years was less satisfying than the journey. The takeaway? Don't pin your happiness on the future. If we can't find ways to feel content here, today, now, we might never feel it.

Stories offer another powerful function: explanation. For this purpose, they aren't usually the main attraction but more the support. And they usually come in the form of short inserts designed to illustrate or reinforce an idea.

Stories resonate deeply in every human. By giving your talk as a story or a series of related stories, you can forge a deep connection with your listeners. But please: let it be true and let it mean something.

PREPARATION PROCESS

7

PREPARATION, NOT PERSPIRATION

Preparation is a key ingredient to alleviating nerves and ensuring your talk's success. Time and again, I've seen this proven by speakers who come to the TED stage.

Once, we had a brilliant physicist come and give a talk about remarkable new developments in the field. His lectures were always packed, and in rehearsal he wowed us with his passion and eloquence and clarity. I couldn't wait for his big moment!

He started out well, striding the stage and capturing the audience right away. And then he lost his way for a moment. He smiled and pulled out his phone to remind himself where he was. Then he moved on. No problem.

Except it happened again forty seconds later. A brilliant metaphor started to confuse rather than clarify. People were scratching their heads, and you could feel the stress growing in the room. His voice tightened. He coughed. I handed him a bottle of water.

For a moment it seemed to help.

But no.

In horrifying slow motion, the talk imploded in front of us. As comedian Julia Sweeney later remarked, it was as if he were disappearing into one of the black holes he was talking about. Out came the phone again—several more times. He began reading from it. The smile and passion had vanished. The water bottle had been sucked dry. Beads of sweat were glistening on his forehead. He sounded like he was choking to death.

Somehow, he got to the end, finishing to a round of awkward, sympathetic applause. His talk was the talk of the conference. But not in the way he dreamed it would be.

Here's the thing: This wasn't his fault. It was mine. In preparing him, I had encouraged him to create a truly blockbuster talk by scripting it out carefully in advance. Most TED speakers use that approach, and it seemed to work well in rehearsal. But it wasn't his natural speaking style.

He had explained that topic masterfully to countless students using spontaneous language straight from his amazing brain. I should have asked him to bring *that* skill to TED. In fact, he *did* bring that skill to TED. Just the prior day, he had come onstage to give a brilliant, off-the-cuff explanation of a major breaking story in physics. It was the scripting that messed him up.

There are many ways to prepare for and deliver a talk, and it's important to find the one that's right for you. Because when it comes to the exact moment, even if you've prepared something that is stunning, a long list of things could go wrong:

You might speak way too quickly.

Or you might run out of time before you've covered half of what you mean to say.

Your classmates might snicker, or ignore you, or hold distracting side conversations.

Something could go wrong with your laptop, slides, or other visual aids.

You could fail to make eye contact with a single member of the audience.

You might forget everything you learned about standing straight and centered, and instead shuffle from foot to foot.

The audience might fail to laugh when it's supposed to.

Or it might laugh when it's definitely *not* supposed to.

Or—the one thing people dread most—you might forget what you were going to say next as your mind goes blank and you freeze.

Why this laundry list of calamities? Two reasons: One, it's helpful to acknowledge that things can and sometimes *do* go wrong; and two, smart preparation not only helps you cope in the face of minor—or major—speaking catastrophes but also lessens the likelihood of things going wrong in the first place.

So how to best prepare? In addition to all the tips about finding your story and throughline, it's also important to know *how* you plan to deliver your talk. Different speakers take different approaches. Some do better with a fully written-out script of a presentation, and some do better with an outline or even old-fashioned index cards.

One of the first key decisions you need to make is whether you will write out the talk in full as a complete script (to be read, memorized, or a combination of the two) or work with an outline of some kind—bullet points to keep you organized and focused but allow you to speak more spontaneously on each point.

There are powerful arguments in favor of each strategy.

SCRIPTED TALKS

It can be tough to condense everything you want—or need—to say on a topic into a brief presentation. Writing out an exact script of your talk and timing it helps you stick to the essential points for exactly the allotted amount of time. It's helpful if you have to convey complex ideas or make a persuasive argument that builds logically from one idea to the next. Scripting also allows you to share drafts of the talk ahead of time to get feedback, allows the audience to read the information in advance, or just creates a transcript for future reference.

As a general rule of thumb, if you're speaking at a non-hurried rate, one double-spaced page of text translates to about two minutes of speaking time. Knowing that can help prevent you from scrambling for content or having to rush through your speech. It can also help you make sure you leave time for questions, if appropriate.

The big drawback of a script is that, unless you deliver it in the right way, the talk may feel stilted. Being read to and being spoken to are two very different experiences. In general, audiences respond far more powerfully to the latter. In other words, the best way to sound like you're not reading a speech is to *not* read a speech.

This is something of a puzzle. If they're the same words, and everyone present knows they were written by the speaker, why should we care how they're delivered to us?

It goes back to all the elements we discussed earlier: eye contact, body language, connection. You say something. I look at your eyes and make all manner of unconscious judgments. Is this something you really mean? Are you passionate about it? Are you committed to it? As a listener, until I know these things, it's too risky to open up my mind to you. That means there's huge power in letting the audience watch you "think out loud" in the moment. We can sense your conviction, and we get to be part of the excitement of seeing a big idea identified, battled with, and finally molded into shape. The fact that we can sense that you truly *mean* what you're saying helps give us permission to embrace that meaning.

Even in cases where your topic is assigned to you as part of class work and you may not actually have a deep personal connection to the material, your audience is still watching for clues that you're prepared and engaged in the topic in some way.

If you go the script route, you have three main strategies open to you:

- Know the talk so well that it doesn't for a moment *sound* scripted.

- Refer to the script but compensate by looking up often to make eye contact with the audience. Notice I didn't say to *read* the script. You may have the entire thing there in front of you, but it's important that you feel as if you're in speaking mode, not reading mode. The audience can tell the difference. It's all about giving meaning to the words, saying them as naturally and passionately as you can. It's about audience eye contact and smiles or other facial expressions. It's about being familiar enough with the script that you're really just glancing down once every sentence or two. Yes, this takes work, but it's worth it, and it's still far less daunting than full memorization.
- Condense the script to bullet points and plan to express each point in your own language in the moment. This has its own set of challenges, covered on page 58 in "Unscripted Talks."

There are only two circumstances in which you might get away with actually reading your script:

- Your talk is accompanied by absolutely gorgeous images or videos that play while you're speaking. In this scenario, the audience's attention is on the screen, and the images are the star of the show, while you're the lyrical caption provider.

- You are a truly great writer, and the audience understands that they are listening to a piece of written work. But as we'll see below, even for great writers with a script in lyrical language, it can be more powerful *not* to read.

The most reliable way to say what you really want to say, in the most powerful and organized way, is to first script it out and get to know it so it's part of you. Sure, that's hard work—both the writing and the memorizing. But it can pay off in terms of your confidence in both the material and your ability to present it.

That said, it's so important to fully prepare so that when you show up in front of your classmates or in front of a larger audience, you're not struggling to remember a script.

When that happens, the problem is not so much the risk of a total freeze. It's that the audience will be able to *tell* you're reciting. They'll notice your tone is flat and robotic because you're focused on bringing the right sentences out instead of bringing real *meaning* to those sentences.

This is actually something of a tragedy. You put in all that work to create an amazing talk, but then you never really gave it a chance to have an impact.

Imagine you're helping a friend prepare to give a talk. Each day you ask him to give you the best version of the presentation he can without using notes. Early on in the process, he'll likely be quite convincing, if a little unstructured. He doesn't know the talk by heart yet, so he simply does his best to give you the information he knows, more or less in the order he's planned.

A few days into the process, you'd likely notice a change. Your friend has reached the point where he knows quite a bit of the talk by heart, and so those parts come out in eloquent paragraphs. *But* you don't feel the original liveliness from them. You feel his stress. You hear words like *Let's see; Just a minute; Let me start that again.* Or you simply hear those paragraphs rattled off a little automatically.

If your friend comes to the stage in this mode, his talk won't be as strong. He'd do better to forget about delivering a scripted talk and instead write down seven bullet points and speak a bit about each of them. Or take the script with him to the stage.

Yet if he *persists* in memorizing his talk, by the sixth or seventh day, you'll notice a thrilling change. Suddenly, your friend really knows the talk. Recalling it is a snap, and he sounds much more natural. He's able to focus on the *meaning* of the words again, adding emphasis in the right places, making eye contact, and generally coming across with greater authority. The speech has become a part of him, which makes it much more likely to land powerfully with the audience.

TED speaker and voice artist Rives says, "When I have time to memorize a talk, I memorize the talk until the talk is like a tune. I rehearse the talk until I'm *performing* the talk, not *remembering* it. And good riddance, reciting."

That's the key. Don't think of it as *reciting* the talk. You're supposed to *live* it. Embody it. Your sole goal is to become so well versed that remembering the words is no longer an effort and you can use your stage time to impart passion and meaning to the audience. It should come across as if you are sharing these ideas for the first time.

One other key question for scripted talks is what type of language you should use. Spoken language or written language? The language we use in everyday speech is quite different from the language writers use. More direct, less lyrical.

The advice of most speaking coaches is to stick to spoken language. That way, it can be spoken from the heart, in the moment. It is, after all, a *talk*, not a *write*. Martin Luther King didn't say, "Vivid, powerful, unforgettable is the vision I bring to you this day." He said, "I have a dream."

Harvard professor Dan Gilbert advises his students to speak their talks into a recorder first, then transcribe them and use that as the initial draft of their talk. Why? "Because when people write, they tend to use words, phrases, sentence structures, and cadences that no one uses in natural speech. When you start with written text and then try to adapt it for performance, you are basically trying to turn one form of communication into another."

The exception to this, of course, is if you're actually doing a *reading* of your written work—a poetry slam, for example, or open mic of some kind. In this case, while it's still a good idea to memorize your work, the expectation is that your speech will *highlight* the artfulness of your language. That's really the point of the talk.

As a great example of this, check out the TED Talk by poet Sarah Kay, who has performed spoken-word poetry since the age of fourteen and whose Project VOICE helps others use poetry as a tool of empowerment and literacy.

Sarah never has a lectern in front of her. Never reads from notes. She stands in front of her audience and speaks—sometimes even *sings*—directly to them. She smiles and has full command of the stage because she's memorized her poems and can deliver them from the heart.

If this is the nature of your talk, it's certainly okay to read. But if you go this route, do your audience the honor of *knowing your script* so well that you can still give a sense of *feeling* it in the moment. Mean every sentence. Look up as often as you can and make eye contact. Prepare so thoroughly in advance that if your notes were swept out the window by a surprise breeze, you could carry on to the end with just as much ease and impact.

UNSCRIPTED TALKS

There's a lot to be said for going unscripted. It can sound fresh, alive—*real*. If you're most comfortable speaking this way, and if you're covering material that you're very familiar with, this may be your best bet.

It's important, of course, to distinguish between *unscripted* and *unprepared*. In an important talk, there's no excuse for the latter. Unprepared speakers tend to ramble, miss key elements, offer half-baked ideas, and generally make their audiences feel as though they've wasted their time. And as previously discussed, it's also nerve-racking to stand in front of an audience without proper preparation. Do yourself a favor and don't try to wing it completely!

How do you prepare for an unscripted talk? The key to the process is to go back to the metaphor of the journey and ask yourself what each step of the journey looks like. At a minimum, a label for each step can be your set of bullet points or mental notes.

You also need a strategy to avoid the obvious pitfalls of such an approach:

- **That suddenly you can't find the words to explain a key concept.** Antidote: Practice several versions of each step in your journey until you're confident you have complete mastery of each one.
- **That you leave out something crucial.** It may be worth working on a transition from each step to the next that makes the sequence come naturally. You might also commit to remembering those transition phrases or add them to your notes.
- **That you overrun your time slot**. Your classmates might love you for going long if it means their turn is delayed, but in other venues, it might inconvenience the event organizers or the speakers who come after you. It might also stress out your audience. Don't do it.

- The only antidotes are to: try out the talk several times to be sure it can indeed be done within the time limit (if not, cut the material); keep an eye on the clock or your phone; and prepare a talk that is no more than 90 percent of your time limit.

Where you're accompanying your talk with slides or videos, it may be tempting to use those presentation graphics as an organizational crutch. At their worst, though, they offer the same old boring templates audiences have seen a million times, and they often result in the speaker saying the exact same thing that's onscreen.

Most people by now understand that this is a truly terrible way to give a talk. Every word you speak that someone has already seen on a slide is a word that carries zero punch. It's not news anymore.

Sometimes the use of presentation software is required by your teacher, but that doesn't mean it has to be boring. We'll discuss this in greater detail in a bit, but a well-structured set of slides can help keep your talk moving along. It just has to be done subtly.

For example, you could have a new image that prompts each element in your talk. If you get stuck, advance to the next slide and it should pull you back on track. But note that this isn't ideal. It's better to tease the arrival of a slide before revealing it rather than having slides lead you through your talk.

Frankly, if you're not required to use a particular set of tools, the old-fashioned method of a set of punchy notes handwritten on cards is still a decent way to keep yourself on point. Use the words that will trigger a key sentence or a phrase that launches the next step in your talk.

One thing to understand is that audiences really don't mind one bit if you pause for a moment to take stock and find your place again. You might feel some discomfort. They won't. The key is to be relaxed about it.

When superstar DJ Mark Ronson came to TED, he was masterful at this. He lost his way at one point, but he simply smiled, walked over to a bottle of water, sipped it, told the audience this was his memory crutch, studied his notes, took another sip, and by the time he got going again, everyone liked him even more.

—

TED speakers have vastly different opinions, by the way, on whether a memorized script or a more improvisational approach is the better way to go.

Elizabeth Gilbert is firmly in the former camp.

Memorization makes me feel comfortable and safe; improvisation makes me feel chaotic and exposed. Public speaking, even for those of us who enjoy it, can be frightening, and fear can make you go blank. I would rather risk sounding like I am reciting something from memory than sounding like I lost my way, or like I never had a plan, or like I have no idea what the heck I'm talking about up there.

Singer and author Amanda Palmer agrees:

I'm a master improviser, but talks aren't the place for improvising, especially on a stage like TED where the time limit is so strict. I considered leaving spots where I could let myself muse and waffle a bit, but as I wrote and rewrote and practiced, I realized that I could convey MUCH more meaning if I did the work ahead of time and distilled my forty-second waffle down into a bite-sized, five-second protein pill.

Educator and entrepreneur Salman Khan has a different stance:

Believing what you are saying in real time has a much larger impact than saying the exact right words. I personally tend to list out bullet points of what I want to talk about and then try communicating those ideas in my natural language as if I'm talking to friends at a dinner table.

As you engage in different types of public speaking, you'll find your way. You might want to create talking points for arguments you're making as part of the debate team, but you might want to fully memorize a presentation you're giving for class. You should do whatever makes you comfortable, and that might change from one presentation to the next. That's perfectly fine.

The good news is that whether you memorize meticulously or wing it with abandon, you're aiming for the same horizon: a feeling of time well spent on the part of your listeners.

8

WAIT, I NEED TO REHEARSE?

Musicians rehearse before playing. Actors rehearse before opening the theater doors to the paying public. Yet many speakers seem to think they can just walk onto the stage and get it right the first time. As a teen speaker, you might find that your "stage" is just the classroom, and your talk might be just one assignment in a sea of assignments. That could make it tough to find the time or enthusiasm for rehearsing your talk, but you'll be glad you did.

Stem cell scientist Susan Solomon is passionate about the power of rehearsal:

> By the time you are ready to give your talk, you should have rehearsed it so many times that you feel as if you could do it in your sleep, and in front of any audience. Rehearse in front of friends. Rehearse by yourself. Rehearse with your eyes closed. Rehearse sitting at your desk, but without using your notes. And be sure that, in your rehearsals, you include your visuals, since timing with them is critical.

Even a speaker like science writer Mary Roach, who doesn't believe in scripting and memorizing her talks, still makes a point of rehearsing.

> My talk was not written out word for word or memorized. But it was rehearsed—at least twenty-five times, using ten note cards and a timer. There's a kind of unintentional memorization that develops naturally from repetition. I think that's what you're after. Memorization feels safer, but a little risk is good. Fear is energy, and you want some of that running through your wires.

That phrase *unintentional memorization* is important. If you rehearse enough, you may find yourself simply knowing the talk in its best form.

That's what Clay Shirky does—he prepares for a talk by talking. He says,

> I start with a basic idea, figure out an introductory sentence or two, and then just imagine myself explaining it to people who care about the idea.
>
> In the beginning, the talking is to get a sense of what fits and doesn't fit—it's more editing than rehearsing. After a while, the talking becomes for pacing and timing. And by the end, I'm mostly just talking out the transitions. Slides help, of course, but rehearsing the transitions is especially important. The audience needs to hear

in your voice when you're doubling down on an idea, versus when you're changing subjects.

I always make written notes, but I never write out the talk. Instead, I write down a list of what theater people call beats.

Beats are the important subjects you want to cover, in the order you want to cover them.

But let's acknowledge this: Rehearsals are hard. They're stressful. And they're not terribly exciting. Even committing to a run-through in your bedroom is tough. When you have a ton of homework to do, rehearsals may feel like time you can't afford to take.

But if a talk is important, and unless the topic is absolutely second nature, you really, really owe it to yourself and the audience to rehearse. Rehearsing helps you organize. It can spark inspiration for new ideas you want to share. And most of all, of course, it lends itself to your feelings of confidence and excitement over delivering your talk.

A quick success story: Once upon a time, Bill Gates was considered a poor public speaker. You might think it doesn't matter much. After all, he's *Bill Gates,* one of the richest and most influential men in the world. Does he need to be a perfect speaker? No, he doesn't. But his passion for the issues he wanted to present—philanthropy, public health, energy, and education—fueled his desire to get better at speaking.

Even though he's probably one of the world's busiest people, he started to put a huge effort into learning and rehearsing his talks. By taking preparation seriously, he's become a much more masterful speaker, producing powerful speeches for TED Talks and organizations like the United Nations.

The moral of the story? If it's worth Bill Gates's time to rehearse, it's probably worth your time too.

At first, you might decide to rehearse alone in front of the mirror or to record yourself on the phone and study how you look and sound, what you can make better, what text you might be able to cut. Eventually, though, it's a great idea to bring other people into your rehearsal process: a trusted friend (who'll also tell you the truth) or family member, even a teacher.

Some things to ask your audience during or after these rehearsals:

- Did I grab your attention right away and keep it?
- Was I making eye contact?
- Were there enough examples to make everything clear?
- Did I sound natural and conversational, as compared to stiff or preachy?
- Did I vary my tone and pacing enough?
- Were my attempts at humor natural or awkward? Was there enough humor? Too much?
- How were the visuals? Did they help or get in the way?
- Did you notice any annoying behavior? Did I click my tongue? Shift from side to side? Repeatedly use phrases like "um" or "you know" or "like"?

- Did my body language and gestures seem natural?
- Did I finish on time?

Let's talk about time limits. It's important that you take the clock seriously. This is certainly true when you're part of a packed program like TED, but it's relevant in just about any setting.

When it comes to the actual day of your talk, the last thing you want is to be worried about time. Whether you finish too quickly or go on too long, it's a problem for both you and your listeners. Sometimes it becomes a problem for your grade. But even in other arenas—a workshop or rally, a speech at a place of worship—it can be a problem, throwing off the day's schedule or cutting into another speaker's time. Sticking to the allotted time is not just a matter of efficiency but of courtesy as well.

On the day itself, if you know you're going to be okay on time, it will allow you to focus 100 percent on the topic you should be focused on—and the people with whom you're sharing your ideas.

9

PRESENTATION PROPS

PowerPoint. Prezi. Google Slides: As a teen, you may have no choice of presentation software and whether or not to use it. Some schools—or teachers—prefer or even *insist* on a particular selection. For some presentations, you may be asked to memorize facts on a topic with absolutely no audio/video aids at your command. For others, you might be directed to use note cards only.

However, there will be instances when you're talking before a larger, public audience—for example, at a conference or in your place of worship—where you'll have greater control over the applications and technology you use for your talk. It's helpful to get acquainted with all different kinds of software to find out which ones you like best and can use with the greatest ease.

For the purposes of this chapter, we're going to assume you have access to some presentation software and are in an arena where its use is appropriate. Your A/V might provide the backdrop for a poetry reading or a video you're creating for your YouTube channel.

Whatever the case may be, we're living in an amazing time when we have the ability to bring our spoken words to life with a dazzling array of technologies that, done right, can take a talk to a whole new level.

When you *do* have the choice of whether or not to add multimedia elements to your talk, the first consideration should be: Will they add or subtract?

Surely a talk plus images is always going to be more interesting than just a talk, right? Well, no, actually. Slides shift at least a bit of attention away from the speaker and onto the screen. If the power of a talk is in the personal connection between speaker and audience, slides or video may actually get in the way of that. And for every speaker, the following is true: Having no slides at all is better than having bad slides. Still, many talks do benefit from great slides, and for some presentations, the visuals are the absolute difference between success and failure.

Of course, TED was originally a conference devoted purely to technology, entertainment, and design, with a result that many presentations featured elegant, impactful media along with stirring talks.

So what are the key elements to strong visuals? They fall into three categories: **revelation**, **explanation**, and **appeal**. Let's handle those in turn.

REVEAL!

The most obvious case for visuals is simply to show something that's hard to describe. Describing a Picasso painting in words is a lot less effective than putting it up on a screen in front of your audience.

Dr. Edith Widder was part of the team that first captured the giant squid on video. When she came to TED, her entire talk was built around that moment of revelation. When the incredible creature appeared onscreen, the audience nearly jumped out of its skin. Widder could have tried to describe this amazing creature in words, but nothing compared to actually seeing its first teasing dance, followed by the full reveal of an entity as big as a two-story house.

Of course, the use of images for revelation doesn't have to be as dramatic. The key is to set the context, prime the audience, and then *BAM!* Let the visuals work their magic. Run them full-screen, with minimal adornment.

EXPLAIN!

A picture is worth a thousand words (even though it takes words to express that concept). But often, the best explanations happen when words and images work together—when you both tell *and* show.

For that to work, there needs to be a compelling fit between what you tell and what you show. Don't overwhelm the audience with too many images or words on a slide. Limit each slide to a single core idea. Where it makes sense to do so, consider whether anything more can be done with a slide to highlight the point it's trying to make.

This is especially true with graphs and charts. If you're talking about how rainfall in February is always greater than in October, and you show a graph of annual rainfall, why not give the audience the gift of highlighting February and October in different colors? And if you then go on to make a comparison between March and November, do that with a separate slide with those months highlighted. Don't cram it all on one slide.

Some speakers still seem to believe that you enhance the explanatory power of your slides by filling them with words, often the same words you plan to utter. Nothing could be further from the truth. Those generic PowerPoint slides with a headline followed by multiple bullet points (shudder!) are sure to lose the audience's attention. Why? Because the audience has already read ahead of the speaker, and by the time the speaker covers a specific point, the audience is already anxious to move on.

The point is there is no value in simply repeating in text what you are saying onstage. Conceivably, if you are developing a point over a couple of minutes, it may be worth having a word or a phrase onscreen to remind people of the topic at hand. But otherwise, you want the words on the screen to *enhance* your presentation, not fight it. And you never want to commit the sin of being *boring*.

Even when a text slide is simple, it may be indirectly stealing your thunder. Instead of a slide that reads: *A black hole is an object so massive that no light can escape from it*, you'd do better with one that reads: *How black is a black hole?* That way, the slide teases the audience's curiosity and makes your words *more* interesting, not less.

To put it simply, the main purpose of visuals can't be to communicate words. Your mouth is already good at that. It's to share things your mouth can't do so well: photographs, video, animations, music, key data.

Used this way, the screen can explain in an instant what might take hours otherwise. One great example is the TED Talk "Are Athletes Really Getting Faster, Better, Stronger?" by sports-science reporter David Epstein. His talk uses striking visual comparisons of athletes and the physical changes they've undergone over the years. The images add to his speech rather than just presenting it in a different format.

So when you're creating visuals for your presentation, it's important to ask yourself: *Are visuals key to explaining what I want to say? And if so, how do I best combine them with my words so that they're working powerfully together?*

DELIGHT!

Sometimes the strongest case for adding visuals is to delight your audience. This can be done in so many ways, but the basic idea is to surprise, thrill, or just plain tickle (not literally, of course) the viewer. This can be done by providing an amusing contrast between what you're saying and the images on the screen. Or it can be done by taking the audience on a "wonder walk" through the world of an unfamiliar artist or culture.

In her TEDxTeen talk, then-fifteen-year-old Tavi Gevinson, fashion blogger and feminist, used purposely homespun images to underscore her point that she, like many teens, is just trying to "figure it out." And in his collaborative talk with twelve-year-old scientist Amy O'Toole, neuroscientist Beau Lotto used a viral video of a frog attempting to eat flies pictured on an iPhone screen to demonstrate the concept of frustration.

A tour through many of the TED Talks mentioned here will treat you to funny, awesome, delightful videos—featuring Tim Urban's Instant Gratification Monkey, Ze Frank's Web Playroom, and, of course, the first appearance of Edith Widder's friend, the giant squid.

The great thing about delightful visuals—and presentation visuals in general—is that they don't have to be limited in the way your actual speech does. Not every graphic needs to be explained. With images, a five-second viewing, even without any accompanying words, can have impact. If it's so easy to offer such a gift to the audience, why withhold it?

To explore some core principles of great visuals, I'd like to invite TED Community Director Tom Rielly to the page.

TOM RIELLY: Great! Let's start with the tools you'll use.

PRESENTATION-SOFTWARE TIPS

Whatever presentation software you like—or are required—to use, please don't use the software's built-in templates of bullets, letters, and dashes. Your presentation will look the same as everyone else's, and the templates end up being limiting.

I recommend you start with a totally blank slide. If you're showing a lot of photos, use black as the background. It will disappear, and your photos will pop.

Most photographs should be shown "full bleed." That's not a horror-movie term but an old printing term meaning that the image covers the entire screen. Better to have three full-bleed photos in a row than three images on one slide.

Photo resolution: Use pictures with the highest resolution possible to avoid annoying pixilation of the images when projected on large screens. There is no such thing as too high a resolution, unless it slows the software down.

FONTS/TYPEFACES

It's usually best to use one typeface per presentation. Some typefaces are better suited to slides than others. We usually recommend sans serif fonts like Helvetica, Arial, or Calibri. *Sans serif* means the letters don't have flourishes on the end intended to guide the eye from one letter to the next, like Times New Roman or other fonts meant for body text rather than headings.

Don't use excessively thin fonts, as they are hard to read, especially on a dark background. If in doubt, keep it simple. Comic Sans and Papyrus are strictly forbidden.

Font size: Tiny type causes the audience to struggle to read it. Use twenty-four-point or larger in most cases. Use *at most* three sizes of your chosen typeface per presentation, and there should be a reason for each size. Large size is for titles/headlines; medium size is for your main ideas; small size is for supporting ideas.

Font background: The background on which your text is displayed can mean the difference between legible and impossible to read. If you're going to place type over a photo, make sure you place it where your audience can read it. If a photo is too busy to put type on directly, add a small black bar at the bottom and put the type on it.

Font color: Here the operative words are *simplicity* and *contrast.* Black on white, a dark color on white, and white or yellow on black all look good because they have great contrast and are easy to read. Use only one color of font per presentation unless you want to show emphasis or surprise. Never use light-color type on a light-color background or dark-color type on a dark-color background. For example, light blue on yellow or red on black will just be tough to read.

LEGIBILITY

After you make your font and color choices, look at your presentation on your laptop or—if you can—on your television or a projector. Stand back six to twelve feet. Can you read everything? Do the photos look clear without pixilation/graininess? If not, readjust.

WHAT NOT TO DO

- Bullets belong in *The Godfather*. Avoid them in presentation slides at all costs.
- Dashes belong at the Olympics, not at the beginning of text.
- Resist underlining and italics. They're too hard to read. Bold typefaces are okay.
- Don't use multiple type effects in the same line. It just looks terrible.

EXPLANATIONS AND DIAGRAMS

Use builds, which means adding words and images to a slide through a series of clicks, to focus people's attention on one idea at a time. Give your audience enough time to absorb each step. Don't feed too much of the slide at a time, or people will get overwhelmed. And again, don't just lay out on the slide what you're saying in your presentation.

PHOTO CREDITS

For school presentations, the issue of photo credits may be less critical than if you bring your talks into other arenas. But as a general rule, it's smart to get into the habit of crediting the sources from which you get your photos—along with making sure you have permission to use those photos in the first place.

It can be illegal, for example, to pull an image from a website without knowing for certain that it's okay to use.

Your presentation software might offer its own images for you to use freely, or you might tap into an online resource, like Pixabay, which offers member-uploaded images, free for use and with no need for credits.

If you do need to include credits, they should be positioned and styled consistently, in the same place, same font, same size (no more than ten-point) on every slide.

As for format, it can be as simple as "Photo Credit: Joe Smith." Or you might be asked to include the institution or periodical that's the source of the photo. Whatever format you use, try to make sure the credit is readable but doesn't overpower the image.

VIDEOS AND GIFS

Videos and GIFs can be amazing tools to demonstrate your work and ideas. However, you should rarely show clips longer than thirty seconds unless they're essential to your talk. While viral video clips or GIFs can seem to be open to public use, it's important to be careful, especially when speaking in any larger arena, not to use clips that shouldn't be used without express permission.

As with still images, also make sure your video plays at a high-enough resolution to be viewable and that it won't crash the computer on which it plays—another reason why shorter clips are better.

TRANSITIONS

Beware the dreaded quicksand of excessive transitions. Rule of thumb: Avoid nearly all of them. "Shimmer," "sparkle," "confetti," "twirl," "clothesline," "swirl," "cube," "scale," "swap," "swoosh," "fire explosions," and dropping and bouncing sounds like in 1970s dance tracks are all real Keynote presentation-software transitions. And I never use any of them, except for humor and irony. They are gimmicky and serve to shift focus from your ideas to the mechanics of your software.

There are two transitions I do like: "none" (an instant cut, like in film editing) and "dissolve." "None" (or "cut") is great when you want an instant response to your clicker, and "dissolve" looks natural if it's set to a time interval of less than half a second.

"Cut" and "dissolve" even have two subconscious meanings: With "cut," you're shifting to a new idea, and with "dissolve," the two slides are related in some way. That's not a hard-and-fast rule, but it's valid.

You can use cuts and dissolves in the same presentation. If there is no reason for a transition, don't use one. In summary, your transition should never call attention to itself.

TESTING

With visuals, two kinds of tests are important: human and technical. For human testing, have friends or family members watch your presentation. Key questions to ask: Were they interested in your visual elements and able to follow them with no problem? Did they feel the visuals enhanced, rather than just paralleled, your talk? Did they find humor and/or delight where they were supposed to? Did the visuals raise any questions you need to address?

Equally important is technical testing. Equipment that doesn't work means visuals you can't show. What a waste of hard work that would be! So if you can, test your presentation not just at home but on the actual equipment you'll be using for your talk.

Assuming everything works correctly, ask yourself: *Are the slides crisp and bright? Are the transitions quick enough? Are the fonts correct? Are the photos high-resolution? Do the videos play okay? Are there any technical glitches of any kind?* Running through your talk a lot will help you know if the visuals are reliable.

If you can, always try to find out what kind of computer will be used to show your presentation, whether it can be shown in the same program and with the same fonts you used to create it, and, if your host is using the same software, what version they have. Using your own computer, if you can, offers the lowest risk of all.

SAVE, SAVE, SAVE!

It probably goes without saying—but I'm going to say it anyway. Save your presentation as you work on it and make sure to mark the final version "FINAL" so you don't show up with the wrong version of your presentation on your big day. Store all your drafts as well as your fonts, photos, videos, and sound. Then compress everything into a folder and save that to a USB drive, both for use during your speech (if you're not able to use your own computer) and to have a backup of the presentation in case anything goes wrong. It's much better to save obsessively than it is to lose everything and have to start over again—or worse, have nothing to show when it's time for your speech.

Now back to Chris . . .

CHRIS ANDERSON: Thanks, Tom! Let's give him a round of applause.

I am incredibly excited about the ways in which public speaking may evolve over the coming years—including greater access to presentation technology and to speakers finding their audiences online as well as onstage. Teens especially are already at the forefront of this movement, with podcasts and video channels of their own that are viewed by millions—even tens of millions—of people.

But I do also think it's worth sounding a note of caution. Many of the innovations mentioned above are potentially powerful, but they shouldn't be overused. The basic technology of human-to-human speaking goes back hundreds of thousands of years and is very deeply wired into us. In seeking modern variants, we must be careful not to throw out the baby with the bathwater. Human attention is a fragile thing; if you add too many extra ingredients, the main thrust of a talk may get lost.

Let's embrace a spirit of innovation. There are wonderful opportunities out there to advance the great art of public speaking. But let's also never forget that substance matters more than style. Ultimately, it's all about the idea.

10

OPEN AND CLOSE

At the beginning of your talk, you have about a minute to "hook" your audience, inviting them to lean in mentally, to experience the little thrill of anticipation that tells them you'll be sharing something worthwhile.

You want an opening that grabs people from the first moment. A surprising statement. An intriguing question. A short story. An incredible image. Sometimes the best thing you can do is plant what seems to be a contradiction in your listeners' minds—like the idea that the more choices we have, the less happy we become, or the idea that your mind doesn't always control your body; sometimes it's the other way around. When audiences are presented with such ideas, their brains light up. They look forward to hearing about how something that should be impossible makes perfect sense after all.

—

Here are four ways to stake your claim to the audience's attention.

Deliver a dose of drama. Your first words really do matter. TEDxTeen speaker Eva Lewis launched her powerful speech with the following words: "A bullet flies through my cousin's window, where her head had been sixty seconds prior." Instantly, the audience was riveted. We knew that what came next would carry us into matters of life and death.

And on a lighter note, one TED speaker began his talk by saying, "So, my name is Taylor Wilson. I am seventeen years old, and I am a nuclear physicist." You can bet the audience wanted to hear more.

In planning your opening, ask yourself: If your talk were a movie or a novel, how would it open? What idea would bring the audience up short and hook them as powerfully as if you ran up and clutched them by the collar?

This doesn't mean you *have* to cram something funny or dramatic into the opening sentence. Not everyone is a seventeen-year-old nuclear physicist. But by the end of the first paragraph, something needs to land. Something needs to create surprise and/or meaning in the viewer so that they have no choice but to lean in and listen.

Here's the opening of the original script sent to us by sociologist Alice Goffman:

When I was a freshman in college at the University of Pennsylvania, I took a sociology class where we were supposed to go out and study the city through firsthand observation and participation. I got a job working at a cafeteria on campus, making sandwiches and salads. My boss was an African American woman in her sixties who lived in a black neighborhood not far from Penn. The next year I began tutoring her granddaughter Aisha, who was a freshman in high school.

She's just telling her story in a way that's natural to her, probably in the way it first came to her, which so many of us do. It's like opening the cabinet and taking out the first can of soup you see. Digging a little deeper might yield more delicious results.

In Goffman's case, she kept digging. By the time she got to the conference, she had a revised opening worthy of her passion for her topic.

> On the path that American children travel to adulthood, two institutions oversee the journey. The first is the one we hear a lot about: college. College has some shortcomings. It's expensive; it leaves young people in debt. But all in all, it's a pretty good path . . .
>
> Today I want to talk about the second institution overseeing the journey from childhood to adulthood in the United States. And that institution is prison.

That brilliant framing allowed her to talk about the tragedy of America's incarcerated in a way that demands attention: *Hey, they could have been college kids.*

Of course, it's possible to overdo the drama and actually lose people. Maybe you want to connect with the audience a little before hitting them with a dramatic thunderbolt. And you certainly don't want to oversimplify what you're going to talk about. But, done right, this is a compelling way to get a talk started.

Ignite curiosity. If I offered you the chance to hear a talk on parasites, I'm guessing you might decline. But only because you haven't met science writer Ed Yong. Here's how he opened his talk:

> A herd of wildebeests, a shoal of fish, a flock of birds. Many animals gather in large groups that are among the most wonderful spectacles in the natural world. But why do these groups form? The common answers include things like seeking safety in numbers or hunting in packs or gathering to mate or breed, and all of these explanations, while often true, make a huge assumption about animal behavior, that the animals are in control of their own actions, that they are in charge of their bodies. And that is often not the case.

He goes on to describe a species of shrimp whose actions are dictated by the parasites that live inside them. These parasites compel the shrimp to huddle together. Why? Because a *clump* of shrimp is much more visible to the flamingos who *eat* the shrimp. The parasites want to move to more spacious flamingo bellies, where they can, presumably, live their best parasite lives.

Whaaat? Isn't that kind of like *zombie shrimp?* Can nature really do that? How? Why? What does this mean?

Curiosity is interest on fire.

If you want your talk to build an idea in the minds of your audience, curiosity provides the fuel to do so. Neuroscientists talk about questions creating a "knowledge gap" that the brain fights to close. The way for an audience to close that gap is to pay close attention to the speaker. That's when you've got them.

As TEDx speaker and journalist Dan Moulthrop says, "Asking a good question is sort of executing the act of curiosity. Curiosity begins with a thought, and typically what follows is a question, and ultimately what follows from that is a lot of learning, and that's really what curiosity is all about."

So what makes for a good question? Specificity, for one.

How do we build a better future for all? Too broad. Too much of a cliché. I'm bored already.

How did this fourteen-year-old girl, with less than two hundred dollars in her bank account, give her whole town a giant leap into the future? Now we're talking.

Sometimes a little illustration can turn a so-so question into full-on curiosity ignition. Here's how philosopher Michael Sandel began:

> Today, there are very few things money can't buy. If you're sentenced to a jail term in Santa Barbara, California, you should know that if you don't like the standard

accommodations, you can buy a prison-cell upgrade. It's true. For how much, do you think? What would you guess? Five hundred dollars? It's not the Ritz-Carlton. It's a jail! Eighty-two dollars a night.

Often, speakers don't ask an explicit question. At least not at first. They simply frame a topic in an unexpected way that clicks that curiosity button.

Here's V. S. Ramachandran:

I study the human brain, the functions and structure of the human brain. And I just want you to think for a minute about what this entails. Here is this three-pound mass of jelly you can hold in the palm of your hand, and it can contemplate the vastness of interstellar space. It can contemplate the meaning of infinity and it can contemplate itself contemplating on the meaning of infinity.

Are you intrigued? I am. Curiosity is the magnet that pulls your audience along with you. If you can wield it effectively, you can turn even difficult subjects into winning talks.

～

Show a compelling slide, video, or object. Sometimes the best opening hook is a glorious, impactful, or intriguing picture or video.

A twelve-year-old Maasai boy, Richard Turere, began his talk with slides that accompanied these words:

This is where I live. I live in Kenya, at the south parts of the Nairobi National Park. Those are my dad's cows at the back, and behind the cows, that's the Nairobi National Park. Nairobi National Park is not fenced in the south widely, which means wild animals like zebras migrate out of the park freely. So predators like lions follow them, and this is what they do. They kill our livestock. This is one of the cows which was killed at night, and I just woke up in the morning and I found it dead, and I felt so bad, because it was the only bull we had.

Right away, we're brought into Richard's world. And we're introduced to a problem in need of a solution. The promise of that solution, and the engagement with the world of the speaker, sparks our interest.

Twelfth-grade students Miranda Wang and Jeanny Yao offered photographs of the Great Pacific Gyre, also known as the Great Pacific Garbage Patch—an area between Hawaii and California where currents come together, leading to the formation of giant islands of (mostly plastic) debris. Their images illustrated in a powerful and immediate way how harmful plastics are for our environment.

This picture you see here is the Great Pacific Gyre . . . a floating island of plastic waste. Right now, the ocean is actually a soup of plastic debris, and there's nowhere you can go in the ocean where you wouldn't be able to find plastic particles.

It's one thing to hear or read about the devastation plastics cause to the environment and to marine life, but images drive that point home even more potently.

Luckily, these amazing scientists wanted to do more than merely acknowledge the problem. Like Richard, they wanted to solve it, and their desire to do so led them through an incredible scientific journey, ending with the discovery of bacteria that could be cultivated to break down this debris.

But they began with an arresting image that they knew would demonstrate the urgency of the situation and draw audience interest and investment.

Depending on your material, you might play with any number of intriguing starts:

The image you're about to see changed my life.

I'm going to play you a video that, at first viewing, may seem to be impossible.

Here's my opening slide. Can you figure out what this thing is?

Find the one that feels right for you. Compelling, but also authentic. An opening that will boost your own confidence going into the talk.

Tantalize, but don't give it away. Some speakers give away too much, too soon. "Today, I'm going to explain to you that curiosity is the key to an effective presentation." Obviously, I'm sold on this idea, but our hypothetical speaker may have already lost the audience. They think they know the talk already. They're lulled before the speaker even gets started.

Imagine instead that the talk began, *Over the next few minutes, I plan to reveal what I believe is the key to success as a speaker and how anyone here can cultivate it. You'll find clues to it in the story I'm about to tell.* You'll probably give that speaker at least a few more minutes of your attention.

Instead of giving away the content of your talk up front, make a promise about what that content will *offer the listener.* Just make sure, of course, that what you promise they'll receive is of actual interest to them.

As a kid, for example, I hated being dragged out on walks. My parents would say, "Let's go for a hike. We'll get to see a beautiful view of the valley." But six-year-old me didn't care about views, which meant I'd spend every minute whining until we returned home.

Later, they got wise and went for a more cleverly crafted pitch. "We've got a treat for you. We're going somewhere special where you can launch a paper airplane into five miles of empty space." As a fan of anything that flew, I was out the door before they were. It was the same walk.

It's okay to save the big revelations for the middle or end of your talk. In the opening sentences, your only goal is to give your audience a reason to step away from their comfort zone and accompany you on an eye-opening journey of discovery.

As film director and TV show creator J. J. Abrams pointed out in his TED Talk on the power of mystery, the movie *Jaws* owes a lot to the fact that director Steven Spielberg hid the shark for the first half of the movie. You knew it was coming, for sure. But its invisibility helped keep you on the edge of your seat. As you plan your talk, try to channel your inner Spielberg.

If you decide to tease a little, please note that it's still important to indicate where you're going and why. You don't have to show the shark, but we do need to know it's coming. Every talk needs a road map—a sense of where you've been, where you are, and where you're going. Your audience wants to know the shape of the container, even if the contents will be revealed a little at a time.

In crafting your own opening, you can draw inspiration from any or all of the above. You can also build in some of the other techniques covered in the book: tell a story, maybe, or get people laughing. The key is simply to find a good fit for you and for what you're talking about. Just bear in mind that your goal is to persuade someone, in only a few moments, that your talk is going to be a worthy investment of their attention. And then you and your fully engaged audience will be on your way together.

FINISH, DON'T FIZZLE

Where your opening might be considered the invitation to the journey, your ending dictates how people feel about the trip. What knowledge do they carry away with them? What feeling? What will echo in their hearts and minds days, weeks, months, even years later?

It's amazing how many talks simply fizzle. And how many more go through a series of false endings, as if the speaker can't bear to leave the stage.

Here are a few better ways to end:

Call to action. If you've given your audience a powerful idea, why not end by nudging them to act on it? In her TEDxWomen talk, fourteen-year-old Google Science Fair winner Lauren Hodge ended her speech with this request:

> If each one of us takes initiative in our own home, in our own school, and in our own workplace, we can make a huge difference. I want you to reimagine a world with better air quality, better quality of life, and better quality of living for everyone, including our future generations.

In his talk on public shaming, author Jon Ronson's final call to action was admirably succinct: "The great thing about social media was how it gave a voice to voiceless people, but we're now creating a surveillance society, where the smartest way to survive is to go back to being voiceless. Let's not do that."

Personal commitment. It's one thing to call on the audience to act, but sometimes speakers score by making a giant commitment of their own. For instance, the swimmer Diana Nyad gave a TED Talk in which she described how she had tried to do what no one had ever achieved: swim from Cuba to Florida.

On three occasions, Nyad had tried, sometimes lasting for up to fifty hours of constant swimming, braving dangerous currents and near-lethal jellyfish stings. All three times, she failed.

But at the end of her talk, she electrified the audience by saying,

> That ocean's still there. This hope is still alive. And I don't want to be the crazy woman who does it for years and years and years, and tries and fails and tries and fails and tries and fails . . . I can swim from Cuba to Florida, and I *will* swim from Cuba to Florida.

Sure enough, she returned to the TED stage two years later to describe how, at age sixty-four, she'd actually done it.

Taking another look. Sometimes speakers find a way to neatly reframe the case they've been making. Musician Amanda Palmer, who has challenged the music industry to rethink its business model, ended this way: "I think people have been obsessed with the wrong question, which is, 'How do we *make* people pay for music?' What if we started asking, 'How do we *let* people pay for music?'"

Giving listeners a final, fresh perspective on the topic will prompt them to consider your words long after you've finished your talk.

Coming full circle. A carefully constructed talk can deliver a pleasing conclusion by linking back to its opening. Author Steven Johnson began his talk on where ideas come from by revealing the significance of coffeehouses in industrial

Britain. They were places where intellectuals gathered to spark off one another. Toward the end, he told the powerful story of how GPS was invented, illustrating all his points on how ideas emerge. And then, brilliantly, he threw in the fact that GPS was probably used by everyone in the audience that week to do things like . . . find their nearest coffeehouse. You can hear in the audience a little gasp of appreciation and applause at the satisfying way the narrative has come full circle.

Artful exits. Sometimes, if the talk has opened people up, it's possible to end with poetic language that taps deep into matters of the heart. This isn't for everyone, but when it works, it's quite beautiful. Here's how Brené Brown ended her talk on vulnerability.

> This is what I have found [to be important]: To let ourselves be seen, deeply seen, vulnerably seen; to love with our whole hearts, even though there's no guarantee . . . to practice gratitude and joy in those moments of terror, when we're wondering, *Can I love you this much? Can I believe in this passionately? Can I be this fierce about this?* Just to be able to stop . . . and say, "I'm just so grateful, because to feel this vulnerable means I'm alive."

Again, this isn't for everyone, and it's not for every presentation. Though the blobfish might make an excellent topic for your science report, it's probably not necessary to wax poetic about it. But in the right hands and at the right moment, these closings can be transcendent.

An elegant closing paragraph, followed by a simple "Thank you," offers the best shot at a satisfying end to your efforts. Whichever way you end, make sure it's planned. Finish. Don't fizzle.

11

BATTLING THE MONKEY

If you're a human being with a pulse, you've probably had some experience with procrastination. You know, that awesome process of watching days slip by between when you're given an assignment and when you actually start working on it. If this is a habit for you, then you'll know all about the panic, the sleepless nights, the caffeine inhalation, and the feeling that maybe, just maybe, if you gave yourself more time, you could do better work.

As mentioned earlier, many of us think of ourselves as "high-functioning procrastinators" or tell ourselves that we do our best work in a blind rush. But is that really true?

Blogger Tim Urban told a great story during his TED Talk about his experience in college working on his senior thesis, which he was given a year to complete. But he procrastinated so badly, he ended up writing ninety pages in seventy-two hours. He said,

A week later I get a call, and it's the school . . . And they say, "We need to talk about your thesis. It's the best one we've ever seen."

That did not happen.

It was a very, very bad thesis.

You might really be a phenomenal procrastinator, but eventually you're going to turn in a very bad thesis or term paper or be caught without answers during class. Or you might give a rambling, unformed talk that will feel like absolute torture because you're unprepared.

People who are chronic procrastinators, Tim Urban says, wage a constant battle between the Rational Decision Maker and the Instant Gratification Monkey.

Our Rational Decision Maker has a lot of smart things to say, like, "Hey, if you start preparing for this talk now, it will probably turn out a lot better." And, "Are you sure you want to spend this time surfing Instagram for pictures of puppies in raincoats right now?" To that, of course, the Instant Gratification Monkey says, "Heck, yeah, I do."

So why do we do it? Why give all our power to the Instant Gratification Monkey when we know he's like that one friend who just wants company in doing dumb stuff?

One answer might surprise you: fear. Sometimes our anxiety about beginning a project, doing research, spending time working on it, and feeling unsure of how well we're carrying out the assignment can make us feel frozen.

We may not even be aware that we feel this way. We just know that whenever we face the blank page or computer screen, Instant Gratification Monkey swings by to show us something weird on YouTube.

There's an expression: "Feel the fear, but do it anyway." Just as it's okay to be nervous about speaking in public, it's okay to be afraid of putting your presentation together. It can feel overwhelming having to research a person or topic, organize all the information, and prepare notes or a presentation. But if you can acknowledge that fear and find a way of breaking the process into bite-size pieces, you'll be so much better for it in the end.

Writers sometimes talk about "keeping their hands in," meaning that it's important to stay connected to their projects, even if they have only ten minutes a day for the work. The tiniest amount of progress is still progress, and it's much better to touch down in the world of their stories for even the briefest moment than to let the story grow cold and to face the blank page feeling as if they have to start from square one.

The same may be true for you. To start, it's okay to commit to just ten minutes of work on your presentation. Maybe the next day it's twenty. And then forty, and so on. The Instant Gratification Monkey will always be there. Your fun will just feel *better earned* if you take time for your speech. And you'll be able to give a more thoughtful, in-depth talk as a result.

A few other techniques for combating procrastination:

Work in short bursts with rewards along the way. It's perfectly acceptable to work for an hour and then take a fifteen-minute break for something fun. Or to create certain milestones—taking notes on one website, for example—with the promise of a treat at the end.

In fact, if you can begin to associate work with those rewards, you'll find yourself looking forward to it rather than dreading it.

Eliminate distractions. I know, I know. No one wants to hear that smartphones and social media are bad for productivity, but sometimes that's the case. In order to work as efficiently as possible, you might have to put your phone in a drawer or find an app like Freedom or SelfControl, which disconnects you from your favorite sites for an assigned amount of time.

It may be painful at first, but you will get used to it and are likely to find you get so much more done when your phone isn't constantly pinging or when you can't sign onto your favorite procrastination sites.

Make a road map. This is an outline of the work you plan to do and when you plan to do it. Again, give yourself much more time than you think you need. Give yourself a check or a gold star for every day you complete your planned work, and don't forget the rewards along the way.

Pre-work in your mind. At times, we just can't convince ourselves to let the Rational Decision Maker run the show. And that's okay. But what we can almost always do is *think through the work.* This means that even if you're not taking notes or directly working on your presentation, you can start to build details in your mind. Plan what you'd like to say. Ask yourself what information you'll need and where you can find it.

Just as you can mentally rehearse your presentation to make it a success, you can spend time mentally rehearsing gathering your data, pre-writing in your mind, turning over different angles to unearth the most important parts of your speech. Let it start to take shape inside your mind, and you'll find it's a lot easier to put it together when the time comes.

Remember that it's not your job to play with or feed the Instant Gratification Monkey. He'll find other friends, and you'll be better off for it!

ONSTAGE

12

THE ONLY THING YOU HAVE TO FEAR

. . . is public speaking. Because it's scary!

And it's particularly scary because most of us aren't asked to do it all that often. Also, we live in a time when screens provide a comforting distance, a filter between people that allows us a remove from face-to-face responses. With public speaking (in person or online), you get audience feedback, one way or another, pretty immediately.

Young inventor William Kamkwamba talked about his first time on the TED stage in a way many of us would find relatable.

> I had never been away from my home in Malawi. I had never used a computer. I had never seen an internet. On the stage that day, I was so nervous. My English lost, I wanted to vomit.

The good news, for William and for you, is that fear won't kill you. That happens only in bad horror movies. The other good news is that fear is a temporary state. No matter how gross you feel in the hour, day, or week leading up to your big speech, it will be over soon enough, and then you get to surf a wave of sweet relief—at least until you're asked to speak publicly again.

It's also helpful to remember that almost any growing experience comes with a big dose of discomfort. If everyone stayed in their comfort zones, we wouldn't have planes, or great art, or iPhones. Learning to acknowledge and even "lean into" fear can make all the difference in whether or not you succeed in public speaking—and in life.

Of course, you're not alone. Almost everyone has experienced the fear of public speaking. Indeed, surveys that ask people to list their top fears often report public speaking as number one, ahead of snakes, heights—even death.

How can this be? There is no tarantula hidden behind the microphone. You have zero risk of plunging off the stage to your death. Your classmates will not attack you with pitchforks. Then why the anxiety?

Author Glenn Croston suggests that the fear goes way back to our early ancestors and to the need to stay in the good graces of our tribe.

> At a primal level, the fear is so great because we are not merely afraid of being embarrassed or judged. We are afraid of being rejected from the social group, ostracized and left to defend ourselves all on our own.

What others think about us matters hugely—especially to teens, who can feel like they're onstage at all times, being blasted by a megawatt spotlight set on revealing their every imperfection.

But more good news: I've never heard of a case in which a person was kicked out of society or her friend group for being a mediocre public speaker. While it's true that you might be the *first*, it's highly unlikely.

It can be helpful to break down the fear a bit to find out what specifically frightens us: What if you get nervous and stumble over your words? What if you completely forget what you were going to say? Maybe you'll be humiliated! Doing this can give you insight into how to tackle those fears. Scared you'll stumble over your words? Practice your speech even more than you planned to make sure every word comes out exactly as you intended.

Fear triggers our ancient fight-or-flight response. Your body is coiled up chemically, ready to strike or flee. This is measurable physically by a huge rise in adrenaline coursing through your bloodstream.

Adrenaline's great for powering a sprint to safety across the savanna, and it can certainly bring energy and excitement to your presentation. But too much of it is a bad thing. It can dry up your mouth and tighten your throat. Its job is to turbocharge your muscles, and if your muscles are not being used, the adrenaline rush may start them twitching, hence the shaking associated with extreme cases of nerves.

In his TED Talk, singer Joe Kowan talked about one of his first times getting ready to perform onstage.

Now, when you experience fear, your sympathetic nervous system kicks in. So you have a rush of adrenaline, your heart rate increases, your breathing gets faster. . . . Next, your mouth gets dry, and blood is routed away from your extremities, so your fingers don't work anymore. . . . That condition is not conducive to performing folk music. I mean, your nervous system is an idiot. Really? Two hundred thousand years of human evolution, and it still can't tell the difference between a saber-toothed tiger and twenty folksingers on a Tuesday-night open mic?

This is everyone's public-speaking nightmare, right? These are the fears that can keep you up at night. That even make you consider taking an F rather than doing this terribly scary thing. But with the right mindset, you can use your fear as an asset. It can be the driver that persuades you to properly prepare your talk. Reframed, it can be a source of energy and excitement. It can make your speech that much more powerful, and it can help teach you just how brave you can be.

Joe wanted to report that he beat his stage fright like many people do—through practice. But that wasn't the case. It wasn't until he acknowledged it, then wrote and started performing a song about it, that he broke through the fear.

The answer, for Joe, was to be himself and to bring the audience into his feelings rather than trying to hide or work around them. Authenticity, humor, and a willingness to be vulnerable can often take you right through the fear and out the other side to success.

—

Earlier, I talked about a twelve-year-old Maasai boy named Richard Turere who had come up with a surprising invention. His family raised cattle, and one of the biggest challenges was protecting them at night from lion attacks. Richard had noticed that a stationary campfire didn't deter the lions, but walking around and waving a torch seemed to work. The lions were apparently afraid of moving lights!

Richard had taught himself electronics by messing around with parts taken from his parents' radio. He used that knowledge to devise a system of lights that would turn on and off in sequence, creating a sense of movement. It was built from scrapyard parts—solar panels, a car battery, and a motorcycle indicator box. He installed the lights and—presto!—the lion attacks stopped.

News of his invention spread, and other villages wanted in. Instead of seeking to kill the lions as they had done before, they installed Richard's "lion lights." Both villagers and pro-lion environmentalists were happy.

It was an impressive achievement, but at first glance, Richard seemed an unlikely TED speaker because he was painfully shy. It was hard to imagine him on a stage in California in front of fourteen hundred people.

Nevertheless, Richard's story was so compelling that we invited him to come and give a TED Talk. In the months before the conference, we worked with him to frame his story—to find the right place to begin, and to develop his throughline.

Because of his invention, Richard had won a scholarship to one of Kenya's best schools, where he had the chance to practice his talk several times in front of a live audience. This helped build his confidence so that his personality could shine through.

Richard got on an airplane for the first time in his life and flew to Long Beach, California. As he walked onto the TED stage, you could tell he was nervous, but that only made him more engaging.

As Richard spoke, people were hanging on his every word, and every time he smiled, the audience melted. When he finished, people stood and cheered.

Richard's tale, and Joe's, can encourage us all to believe we might be able to give a decent talk. Your goal is not to be Oprah or Barack Obama. It's to be you. Even the slightly (or tremendously) freaked-out version of you. If you know how to talk to a group of friends over lunch, then you know enough to speak publicly.

Everywhere you look, there are stories of people who were terrified of public speaking but found a way to become really good at it, from business leaders like Richard Branson and Warren Buffet to actors like Samuel L. Jackson and Julia Roberts, who turned to their profession to help them overcome their fears.

Another TED participant, Megan Washington, has found her way as a public speaker despite a pronounced stutter. She says:

> I have a problem. It's not the worst thing in the world. I'm fine. I'm not on fire. I know that other people in the world have far worse things to deal with, but . . . the thing is that I have a stutter. It might seem curious, given that I spend a lot of my life on the stage. One would assume that I'm comfortable in the public sphere and comfortable here, speaking to you guys. But the truth is that I've spent my life up until this point, *and including this point,* living in mortal dread of public speaking.

Again, Megan Washington acknowledges her fear, but she doesn't let it stop her. She confides in her audience and wins their sympathy—all the better to help her ideas hit home.

13

SCARING OFF MOUNTAIN LIONS
(AND OTHER HACKS TO
HELP YOU FEEL LESS ANXIOUS)

In parts of the world where mountain lions make their home, hikers are taught that if they ever encounter one of these animals out in the wild, they should "get big" by raising their arms, creating as large a presence as possible while shouting at the animal and, of course, backing away very, very slowly. "Remember," the advice goes, "never bend down or crouch under any circumstance, as it will make you look like . . . delicious prey to the mountain lion."

No one wants to look like delicious prey to a mountain lion, right? Instead, you want to seem larger than you are, like someone a big wildcat should think twice about messing with. What you definitely don't want to do is present as a small tasty morsel. This is helpful advice for the public speaker as well.

In her hugely successful TED Talk, social psychologist Amy Cuddy introduced the idea of "power posing" to the world. Her belief is that not only do our mental states have an impact on our bodies, but what we do with our *bodies* has an impact on our *minds*. When we're anxious or afraid, we tend to shrink our bodies, try to take up less room—almost become invisible. This has the result of making us feel timid and insignificant. It also invites others to see us that way.

But if we can train our bodies into *acting* as though we feel self-assured, our minds will often follow.

Cuddy says,

> [When] you make yourself big, you stretch out, you take up space, you're basically opening up. This is true across the animal kingdom. . . . And humans do the same thing. They do this both when they have power sort of chronically, and also when they're feeling powerful in the moment. . . . What do we do when we feel powerless? We do exactly the opposite. We close up. We wrap ourselves up. We make ourselves small.
>
> We tend to forget [that we're influenced by our own physical behavior]. . . . For example, we smile when we feel happy. But also when we're forced to smile by holding a pen in our teeth, it makes us feel happy. It goes both ways. When it comes to power, it also goes both ways. When you feel powerful, you're more likely to [demonstrate it physically], but it's also possible that when you *pretend* to be powerful, you are more likely to actually *feel* powerful.

Cuddy and her colleagues performed experiments in which people were asked to assume "high-power poses," like standing with their legs spread, hands on their hips, or "lower-power poses," which shrank the body and put people in defensive physical postures. They found that in just two minutes, these poses literally created changes in the mind.

The simplest way to train your body to influence your mind is to stand tall, spread your arms and legs, hands on hips, head held high. Smile and take deep, slow breaths. Act like *I've got this,* because you do!

Here are a few other helpful tips to soothe your jitters and set you up for speaking success.

Let your body help you! The single most important thing you can do before giving your talk is to *breathe.* Breathe deeply, meditation style. The oxygen infusion brings calm with it. You can do this even if you're seated in the audience, waiting to be called up. Just take a deep breath right into your stomach and let it out slowly. Repeat three times more. If you're offstage and you're feeling tension surging through your body, it's worth trying more vigorous physical exercise.

Drink water. The worst aspect of nerves is when the adrenaline sucks the water from your mouth and you struggle to speak. Controlling the adrenaline, as above, is the best antidote, but it's also good to make sure you're fully hydrated. Five minutes before you go on, try to drink a third of a bottle of water. It'll help stop your mouth from getting dry. (But don't do this too early. Salman Khan did and then had to rush to the men's room just before his introduction. He was back in the nick of time.)

Avoid an empty stomach. When you're nervous, eating may be the last thing you want to do, but an empty stomach can exacerbate anxiety. Get some healthy food into your body an hour or so before you're on, and/or have a protein bar handy.

Chew gum. It should go without saying that this is something to do *before* you get in front of people, *not* while you're giving your actual talk. But we're actually hardwired to feel less anxiety when we're eating, presumably so our ancient ancestors didn't topple over in fear every time they heard a twig crack while they feasted on roasted mastodon.

Chewing gum also tricks our body into believing we're supposed to be digesting food, which reroutes some of the adrenaline to become energy and also helps create saliva, so your mouth doesn't go bone-dry during your talk. Again, though, spit it out before you start your speech!

Press your spirit gate. This is an old acupressure trick that's said to relieve anxiety. Find the point on the crease of your wrist straight down from your little finger (called the "spirit gate" in Chinese medicine), and press it firmly with the opposite index finger while taking deep breaths. Do that for a few minutes and then switch to the other wrist. Repeat a few times for best results.

Skip the latte. As painful a thought as this might be, it's best to avoid caffeine on the day of your presentation. Not only can coffee ramp up anxiety; it can also be dehydrating, which can lead to fatigue, fuzzy thinking, and dry mouth. Better to treat yourself *after* your presentation.

Press your desk (or a wall). Another way to calm your nerves is to press your palms against the edge of a desk (imagine you're trying to push the desk away) or against a wall, if you're near one. Pull in your abdominal muscles for bonus points, and don't forget to breathe.

The engagement of your muscles in this way also helps reroute energy in your body so that it's used for what feels like work rather than just floating around as anxiety.

Scrunch those toes. This is a great exercise, especially if you're sitting and waiting to go up in front of the class. Simply scrunch the toes on one foot and then relax them. Then do the same for the other foot. Repeat.

If you're standing, you can do toe scrunches, or you can raise up onto your toes and then lower yourself back down to the ground. Each time you relax after tensing your toes, you'll likely release some anxiety.

Get weird. Before you speak, it can be helpful to remind yourself that your presentation probably isn't a matter of life and death. To do this, it can be great to get out of your head, away from your fear, and just goof around for a bit. That might mean making comical faces in the mirror, jumping around backstage, dancing, or practicing your speech in a silly voice. Whatever you find funny or bizarre: go for it. It will help you release nervous energy, and it will remind you that public speaking is supposed to be a joy, not a punishment.

Step Your Breath: This is a well-known relaxation technique that allows you to put your focus on your breathing. When we're nervous, we tend to forget to breathe deeply and fully, but doing so moves oxygen through our body, which helps reduce anxiety. It also can make us feel calmer and more collected.

For stepped breathing, it's helpful to have one hand on your belly and the other on your chest. When you inhale, the hand on your belly should be pushed forward by your breath. When you exhale, the hand on your chest should move.

If you can close your eyes, that's a plus, but no worries if you can't. Breathe in slowly for five beats, hold your breath for five, and then exhale for seven. Make sure to drop your shoulders. Really fill up with oxygen and go slowly. Breathing in this way may feel awkward at first, or you may feel too nervous to do it, but this technique is excellent for relaxation and focus.

One or more of these techniques is sure to work for you, but remember: it's natural to feel nervous—and okay for others to know you're nervous too. Like author Patrick Allen says, you're "a perfectly normal human being in front of other people." You don't have to be anything other than that.

14

PUTTING YOUR MIND TO IT

Like Joe and Megan (and Samuel L. Jackson!), you may never be fully comfortable speaking in public, but you can make the experience easier by putting your mind to it.

That means putting your considerable brain power to work to challenge the negative and fearful messages it sends you at the thought of giving a speech—or when you're just about to get up in front of people and actually do it!

As with many things, these signals probably go back to our primitive days, when it was smart to feel afraid 99.9 percent of the time. But luckily, your classmates are not tigers or poisonous berries—just other teens like you, with the same fears and doubts swirling in their heads.

In fact, that's battle-your-fear guideline #1: **Remember that your audience is made up of people who, in large part, fear public speaking as much as you do.** They are much likelier to be nervous on your behalf than they are to be judging you.

The old advice used to be to imagine your audience in its underwear, but a) that's weird; b) if you could muster the focus to do it, you'd likely be distracted; and c) it's weird.

Probably the intent of that advice is to take some of the power away from your audience, to make them seem less intimidating and more vulnerable, putting you in a position of strength, which should make you feel more comfortable.

That's a great idea, but your listeners can keep their clothes on. What's important, as mentioned, is to recognize that every single person in the classroom with you, across the desk, or in the crowd *is* vulnerable, is fearful of *something,* if not public speaking. They're just people like you, with good days and bad, hopes and dreams, failures and successes. The only power they have over you is the power you give them.

Which brings me to guideline #2: **If you're going to imagine what people think of you, imagine they're all really impressed.**

Psychologists have a word for the practice of putting thoughts in other people's heads: projecting (also mind reading). You know how sometimes you're sure your best friend is mad at you, and then it turns out he's just annoyed that he flunked his midterm? That's projecting. It's making assumptions about other people's thoughts and feelings without any real evidence to support those assumptions.

The trick is that a good public speaker has to do *some* projecting. He tries to pick up on audience cues to measure the success of the talk as it's being given—and certainly afterward as well. *Which comments receive laughs? Where do I really feel the crowd's full attention?* There's an energy that flows back and forth between audience and speaker, and a good presenter feels and tries to adjust to that energy.

However, we're not always right about what we're feeling—or what we think our audience is feeling. And the less sure we are of our speaking abilities, the more likely we are to assume a negative response from our audience. We feel judged, or laughed at, or like we're boring people.

But it's all really a guess—and a guess that has at least a 50 percent chance of being flat-out wrong. Half the people in the audience might be mentally rehearsing the talks *they're* about to give. And the other half might be thinking about lunch.

If you're going to assume what people are thinking, then why not imagine they're all thinking about the great job you're doing? About the exciting ideas you've just presented? Why not imagine they can't wait to talk to you about how they can become as great a speaker as you?

Guideline #3: **Remember the power of vulnerability.** Audiences embrace speakers who are nervous, especially if the speaker can find a way to acknowledge it. If you flub or stutter a little in your opening remarks, it's fine to say, "Oops, sorry; a little nervous here." Or, "As you can see, I don't do a lot of public speaking." Your listeners will sympathize and root for you even more.

Guideline #4: **Reframe fear as excitement.** That adrenaline you feel? The shallow breathing? The tingling fingers and thudding heart? You experience the same sensations when you're excited as you do when you're afraid. So why not repackage that anxiety as anticipation, that dread as eagerness?

How do you do that? Basically, by talking yourself into it. Whenever you think, "I'm so nervous," try to replace that thought with, "I'm so excited." If you want to go further with your pep talk, practice thinking (even saying aloud), "I'm so excited to give this amazing talk!"

It may feel awkward and cheesy the first time—perhaps even the tenth or twelfth or fiftieth time. But the more you do it, the more instinctive and natural it will become, and the more you'll believe it.

Guideline #5: **Remember your purpose.** In some forms of meditation, you're told to return to your breath or to your mantra (a word or phrase you repeat silently) whenever your mind wanders or "monkey mind" sets in. Do that with your anxiety. If you're going to stand on a stage, addressing an audience, it means someone, somewhere decided you have something important to offer.

You'll no doubt have your own purpose in giving your talk. It's important to get back in touch with the "why" of what you're doing. Sure, it may be for a grade sometimes, but even that *why* can be motivational.

Guideline #6: **The better prepared you are, the less nervous you'll be.** Often our fear of public speaking comes from being underprepared and unsure of the material. Taking your time to research and develop your talk, to figure out how you like to work—with a loose outline or the entire speech on a phone or tablet (or good old-fashioned note cards)—to rehearse in front of family or friends, all of it will help you feel more on top of the information and more confident in your ability to deliver it.

I'll get into the specifics of preparation a bit later, but the key here is just to do it. Even if you're a super-high-functioning procrastinator. Even if you think you do better work when you're cramming. Aside from helping ensure the success of the speech, preparation creates calmness and clarity.

Guideline #7: **Find friends in the audience.** Early on in your talk, try to make eye contact with a friend, family member, or other person who is cheering you on. And if those people aren't in the crowd, look out for faces that seem sympathetic. If you can, find three or four in different parts of the audience and give the talk to them, moving your gaze from one to the next in turn. Everyone else will see you connecting, and the encouragement you get from those faces will bring you calm and confidence.

Lastly, guideline #8: **Visualize success.** This technique can be described as mental rehearsal and is used by Olympic athletes, entertainers, chess masters, and great public speakers alike. When you imagine yourself standing confidently onstage or in front of a classroom, delivering your presentation clearly and with positive results, you train your body and mind to expect it, and you release some of the anxiety along the way.

The more opportunities you give yourself to mentally prepare, to envision every aspect of the event—from the feeling of the venue to the actual words you plan to say—the better off you'll be. As the author Richard Bach says, "To bring anything into your life, imagine that it's already there." This absolutely includes your comfort and success as a speaker.

See it. Believe it. And you can *surely* do it.

15

OWNING YOUR PRESENCE

While studying philosophy in college, I was devastated to find that the wonderful P. F. Strawson, a beautiful writer and brilliant thinker, was, at least on the day I heard him, a truly *terrible* speaker. He mumbled his way through sixty minutes, reading every sentence in the same monotone voice, barely looking up. It felt like a complete waste of time to go to his classes when I could double down on just reading his books. So I stopped going to his lectures. In fact, I stopped going to lectures, period. I just read.

When reading, I could get through pages of a book much more quickly than people could present the same material in a class. I could go at my own pace, backing up or skimming the text as I liked. I didn't have to deal with a speaker's disorganization and note shuffling, his verbal stumbles or silly jokes. I could get at the information the way I wanted to, exactly when I wanted.

It's ironic that, years later, I've grown to believe that talks may offer something more than the printed word. Thanks to TED, I've been educated, moved, and transformed by public speakers far beyond what I've found in books. But it's not a given, and it's not even true in every case. The best speakers, and the speeches that really add up to something memorable for the audience, offer something *extra*. It's the magic that turns *information* into *inspiration*.

On a simple level, we as listeners are receiving information, just as we do when we read a book. But on another level, a public speech offers much more. Our brain functions differently when it is listening and observing than when we read. When a person speaks to us, we respond internally to what we're feeling. For example:

Connection: *I trust this person.*

Engagement: *Every sentence sounds so interesting!*

Curiosity: *I hear it in your voice and see it in your face. Now I'm feeling some of those same feelings.*

Understanding: *The emphasis on that word with that hand gesture—now I get it.*

Empathy: *I can tell how much that hurt you.*

Excitement: *Wow—that passion is infectious.*

Conviction: *Such determination in those eyes!*

Action: *I want to know more—or do more. Sign me up!*

This is inspiration in its broadest sense. I think of it as the force that tells the brain what to do with a new idea. Many ideas just get filed away and soon forgotten. Inspiration, by contrast, grabs an idea and rushes it into our minds' attention spotlight: *General alert! Stand by for important new ideas!*

There are many mysteries in how and why we respond so powerfully to certain speakers. Somewhere inside you resides an algorithm for trust. An algorithm for credibility. An algorithm for how emotions spread from one brain to another. We don't know the details of those algorithms, but we can agree on important clues. And they break down into two big categories: what you do with your *voice* and what you do with your *body*.

SPEAK WITH MEANING

In his TED Talk "How to Speak So That People Want to Listen," sound consultant Julian Treasure says,

> The human voice: It's the instrument we all play. It's the most powerful sound in the world, probably. It's the only one that can start a war or say "I love you." And yet many people have the experience that when they speak, people don't listen to them. And why is that? How can we speak powerfully to make change in the world?

For me, the key takeaway is simply to inject variety into the way you speak, variety based on the *meaning* you're trying to convey.

So many speakers forget this. They give a talk in which every sentence sounds the same—a slight rise at the start and a drop at the end. No pauses or changes of pace. What this communicates is that no single part of your talk matters more than any other part. It's just plodding its way along until it gets to the end. The effect is hypnotic. It puts your audience to sleep.

Julian Treasure suggests keeping in mind the acronym HAIL, which represents "four really powerful cornerstones, foundations, that we can stand on if we want our speech to be powerful and to make change in the world."

> The H, *honesty,* of course, [means] being true in what you say, being straight and clear. The A is *authenticity,* just being yourself. A friend of mine described it as standing in your own truth, which I think is a lovely way to put it. The I is *integrity,* being your word, actually doing what you say, and being somebody people can trust. And the L is *love.* I don't mean romantic love, but I do mean wishing people well.

As has been said here many times, when you're speaking to others, it's best to come at it from a place of generosity, of wanting to get something important across, even if it's just a fascinating tale about the life cycle of a moth. "Wishing people well," as Treasure puts it, means doing your best to speak in a clear and compelling manner.

Take a look at your speech notes and try to find the two or three words in each sentence that carry the most significance. Underline them. Then look for the one word in each paragraph that *really* matters and underline it twice more. Find the sentence that is lightest in tone in the whole script and run a light wavy pencil line under it. Or find some other way to highlight it if it's on your phone, tablet, or computer.

Look for every question mark and highlight each with a yellow highlighter. Find the biggest single *aha* moment of the talk and place a great big black blob on the page right before it is revealed. If there's a funny anecdote somewhere, put little pink dots above it.

Try reading your script, applying a change in tone for each mark. For example, let yourself smile while looking at the pink dots, pause for the big black blob, and speed up a little for the wavy pencil line, while speaking more softly. How does that sound? Silly or contrived? No problem! Try again with a little more nuance. And again, until it feels natural. What's critical is not that you offer a particular intonation at particular points but that you vary the sound of your talk, verbally lean into important ideas.

One more thing: Try to remember all the emotions associated with each passage of your talk. Which are the bits you're most passionate about? Which issues make you a little angry? What are you laughing at? What are you baffled by?

Let *those* emotions out as you speak. How's it sounding? Try rehearsing in front of a friend and see what she responds to and what makes her roll her eyes. Record yourself reading it and then play it back with your eyes closed. Are you varying your tone? Is there musicality in your speech?

The point is to start thinking of your tone of voice as giving you a whole new set of tools to get inside your listeners' heads. You want them to understand you, yes, but you also want them to feel your passion. And the way you do that is not by *telling* them to be passionate about this topic but by showing your *own* passion—a passion you feel because you've found the important story at the heart of your talk.

That passion spreads automatically, as will every other emotion you authentically feel. You can use every second of your talk not just to convey information but to communicate *how* that information might be received. And all without adding a single extra word.

I ask people to imagine they've met up with friends they haven't seen for a while and are updating them on all they've been through. That's the kind of voice you're looking for. Real, natural, but unafraid to let it rip if what you're saying demands it.

One other important aspect to pay attention to: how fast you're speaking. First of all, it's great to vary your pacing according to what you're speaking about. When you're introducing key ideas or explaining something that's complex, slow down, and don't be afraid to insert pauses. During anecdotes and lighter moments, speed up. But overall, you should plan to speak at your natural, conversational pace.

Does that surprise you? Do you think of public speaking as the opposite of conversational speaking?

It's actually a really important point. Public speaking evolved long before the age of amplification. To address a crowd of any size, speakers would have to slow down, breathe deep, and let loose, with dramatic pauses after each sentence. It's a style of speaking we recognize today as *oration*. It can stir up crowd emotions and responses in a powerful way. We associate it with some of the most influential speeches in literature and history, from Marc Antony's "Friends, Romans, Countrymen" to Martin Luther King Jr.'s "I Have a Dream."

In most modern settings, oration is best used sparingly. It's capable of conveying passion and urgency and outrage, but it struggles with the many subtler emotions. And from an audience perspective, it can be deeply moving for fifteen minutes but exhausting for an hour. If you were speaking to a single person, you would not orate. You could not build a daylong conference program around oration.

And oration is much slower. King's famous speech was delivered at around one hundred words per minute. It was perfectly crafted and delivered for its purpose. But it's unlikely that your task today is to address a crowd of two hundred thousand people at the heart of a major social movement. Oration is an art at which only a few truly excel. It can be appropriate in church or at a mass political rally. But for other occasions, I recommend leaving it alone.

Amplification has given us the ability to speak intimately to a crowd. It's an ability worth using. It builds connection and curiosity much more easily than oration. That conversational tone is even more important when you give a talk online. There your audience is a single person looking at a screen, and you as the speaker want to address that person as such.

GIVE YOUR BODY SOMETHING TO DO

Sir Ken Robinson jokes that some professors seem to view their bodies simply as devices to carry their heads into the next meeting. Sometimes a speaker will give the same impression. Once his body has moved his head onto the stage, it no longer knows what to do with itself. The problem is amplified in a setting where there's no lectern to hide behind. People stand awkwardly, hands glued to their sides, or lurch from leg to leg.

The last thing I want to do is dictate what you do with your body. Talks would be really dull if everyone sounded or stood the same way. But here are a few things that may make you feel more comfortable and will better project your authority to your audience.

Straighten up. The simplest way to feel confident and in charge is to stand tall, putting equal weight on both feet, which are positioned comfortably a few inches apart. Don't slouch. Use your hands and arms to naturally amplify whatever you're saying. Don't forget to turn from the waist to address different parts of your audience. You don't have to walk around at all.

Most TED speakers use this method. They stand in one place and invite the audience's attention. The key is to feel relaxed and to let your upper body move as it will. It can be tough and intimidating to just stand and let yourself be seen. It may make you feel like diving under the lectern or running out the classroom door. But that vulnerability works in your favor. It invites people *to* you, which makes them that much more open to your ideas.

Walk the walk. Some speakers prefer to move around while giving their talks. It helps them think. It helps them emphasize key moments. It can even help them release some of their anxiety.

This can work well too, provided the walking is relaxed, not forced. On the TED site, you might take a look at talks by BuzzFeed cofounder Ze Frank or author Elizabeth Gilbert. In both cases, they look extremely comfortable making greater use of the stage. You can tell their movements are natural to them and that they'd feel a lot less comfortable rooted to one spot.

However—and this is important—they do stop here and there to dwell on important points. It's not just that constant pacing can feel frantic and tiring to watch. It's also that there's great power in stillness. It serves as punctuation, creating a mental breath and drawing our attention to the most crucial ideas.

Cut the two-step. Try not to shift from leg to leg while talking or step up and back in a rocking motion. Many speakers do this without realizing it. Often they're feeling anxious, and these movements help ease their discomfort. The only problem is that such movements only *highlight* that discomfort to their audience. Not only that, but such movements may make the *audience* nervous (people are wonderfully empathetic), distracting from the content of your talk. In TED rehearsals we've encouraged speakers to relax and simply stand still. The difference in impact is immediate.

There are no rules here. Move if you want to. But if you do move, move intentionally. And when you want to emphasize a point, stop and address your audience from a stance of quiet power.

Try a few different ways of being onstage. Sit. Stand. Walk. What matters is that you're comfortable and confident, and that your physical behavior onstage underscores—doesn't distract from—what you're saying.

The world can accommodate—and welcome—many different presentation styles. Just make sure your body knows it's not there solely to transport your head. It's allowed to enjoy its own time onstage.

Most important, give your talk in your own authentic way. Don't try to be who your teacher wants you to be. Or your friends or family. Focus on your content and the care you want to give in presenting it. Let your own personality shine through. Because that's what people want to experience: the real and awesome you!

MAKE EYE CONTACT, RIGHT FROM THE START

Generally, humans are great at forming instant judgments about other humans. *Friend or foe. Likable or unlikable. Wise or dull. Confident or tentative.* The clues we use to make these judgments are often shockingly spare. The way someone dresses. How they walk or stand. Their facial expression or body language. Their attentiveness.

Great speakers find a way of making an early connection with their audience. It can be as simple as walking confidently onstage, looking around, making eye contact with two or three people, and smiling.

When eighteen-year-old TEDxTeen speaker Ann Makosinski began her talk on why she doesn't use a smartphone, it was clear she felt a bit nervous. But she found her spot onstage, took a deep breath, and gave her audience a warm smile, one that stayed on her face for most of her presentation. She also made an effort to move her focus around the room, to connect eye to eye with individuals in the audience.

This makes a huge difference in how engaged we feel in a talk. On a subconscious level, we're trained to detect the tiniest movement of eye muscles in someone's face and judge not just how they're feeling but whether or not we can *trust* them. (And while we're doing that, they're doing the same to us.)

Scientists have shown that just the act of two people staring at each other will trigger mirror neuron activity that literally causes one person to adopt the emotional state of the other.

If I'm beaming, I will make you feel lighter inside. If I'm nervous, you'll feel anxious too. If I'm looking into your eyes, you're also taking me in, preparing to bond with me if we seem to be in sympathy with each other. The best way to create that sympathy and trust? A smile. A natural and genuine smile. (I'm sure you've seen some *unnatural* smiles, and those are just . . . creepy.)

At TED, our number-one piece of advice to speakers on the day of their talk is to make regular eye contact with members of the audience. Be warm. Be real. Be you. It opens the door to them trusting you, liking you, and beginning to share your passion.

When you get up in front of your audience, you should think about one thing: your true excitement at the chance to engage with those individuals sitting right there a few feet from you. Don't rush in with your opening sentence. Walk into the light or to the front of the room, pick out a couple of people, look them in the eye, nod a greeting, and smile. Then you're on your way.

SHOW VULNERABILITY

One of the best ways to disarm an audience is to first reveal your own vulnerability. It helps you to meet on the same level. Everyone relaxes.

Author and research professor Brené Brown gave a wonderful talk on vulnerability at TEDxHouston, and she began it appropriately.

> A couple years ago, an event planner called me because I was going to do a speaking event. And she said, "I'm really struggling with how to write about you on the little flyer." I thought, *Well, what's the struggle?* And she said, "Well, I saw you speak, and I'm going to call you a researcher, I think, but I'm afraid if I call you a researcher, no one will come, because they'll think you're boring and irrelevant."

You love her already, because she's willing to poke fun at herself, to find humor where another person might find offense. And she's willing to share that less-than-glowing professional assessment with her audience rather than clinging to some air of superiority.

By the same logic, if you're feeling nervous, it can actually work in your favor. Audiences sense it instantly and, rather than think less of you, they root for you. Many of them have been where you are and feel the same anxiety.

We often encourage speakers who struggle with nerves to just acknowledge it. If you feel yourself choking up, pick up a bottle of water, take a sip, and just say what you're feeling. "Hang in there a moment . . . As you can see, I'm feeling a little nervous here. Normal service will be restored soon."

Willing to be vulnerable is one of the most potent tools a speaker can wield. But as with anything powerful, it should be handled with care. Brené Brown has seen a lot of speakers misinterpret her advice. She told me: "Vulnerability is not oversharing." In other words, it's okay to express your anxiety, and it's even okay to talk about yourself—in some cases you'll be the very subject of your talk. But it's not okay to use your talk as therapy or your anxiety as an excuse to vent. Remember that the best personal talks are ones that offer the listener a lesson learned or some important takeaway. As Brown says, "A story is only ready to share when the presenter's healing and growth is not dependent on the audience's response to it."

Authentic vulnerability is powerful. Oversharing is not. If in doubt, try your talk on an honest friend.

MAKE 'EM LAUGH—BUT NOT SQUIRM!

Humor can be a wonderful way to bring the audience with you. When you laugh with someone, you both feel you're on the same side. Audiences who laugh with you quickly come to like you. And if people like you, they're much more likely to take what you say seriously. Laughter breaks through resistance and leaves an open path for understanding.

Humor can also be an excellent way to disarm people around difficult topics.

Anushka Naiknaware, the youngest winner of the Google Science Fair, was thirteen years old when she gave her TED Talk, which began with her saying, "Ever since I was a young girl . . ." And when the audience laughed, she clarified: "Okay, I mean younger and more short. If that's possible to imagine."

Just as admitting to nervousness or expressing vulnerability in some way can get the audience on your side, humor can as well. It reminds people that education can be engaging and fun, and it makes them want to come with you on the journey you're sharing.

Of course, it's important to find the right tone and level of humor for the audience, content, and purpose of your presentation. Your speech on manifest destiny for AP History is different from an open mic at your local coffee shop. Though you might use humor in both, knowing how to tailor it appropriately can make all the difference between eye rolling and real laughs.

It should generally be the case, too, that you rely less on jokes to bring humor to your talks than on hilarious-but-true stories that are directly relevant to your topic or make endearing, humorous use of language.

The funniest person on our team is Tom Rielly, who for years ran our Fellows program and gave a final wrap-up of the conference that skewered every speaker with wicked hilarity. Here's his advice:

- The best humor is based on observation of things occurring around you and then exaggerating or remixing them.
- Have a funny remark ready if you flub your words, the A/V goes awry, or the clicker doesn't work. The audience has been there, and you'll instantly win their sympathy.
- Build humor into your visuals. You can also have the humor be the contrast between what you're saying and what you're showing. There are lots of great possibilities for laughter.
- Use satire, saying the opposite of what you mean, then revealing your intent, though this is really hard to get right.
- Timing is critical. If there's a laughter moment, you have to give it a chance to land. That may take the

courage to pause for just a moment. And to do so without looking like you're fishing for applause.

- Very important: If you're not funny, don't try to be funny. Test the humor on family or friends, or even a colleague. Are they laughing? If not, change it or spike it.

Dangers (even in the hands of people blessed with the gift of humor):

- Off-color remarks and offensive language: Don't. Even if you get laughs from your friends, your teacher or other adult audience member is unlikely to find the humor in such comments.
- Sarcasm: Even if you can proudly wear the T-shirt that says SARCASM IS MY SUPERPOWER, a very little bit goes a long way in a presentation. Remember that humor is the seasoning, not the substance, of your talk.
- Going on too long: Especially don't let humorous comments turn into formless rambling.
- Any attempted humor based on religion, ethnicity, gender identity, sexual orientation, or politics.

TED speaker Salman Khan put it beautifully:

Be yourself. The worst talks are the ones where someone is trying to be someone they aren't. If you are generally goofy, then be goofy. If you are emotional, then be emotional. The one exception to that is if you are arrogant and self-centered. Then you should definitely pretend to be someone else.

If you plan to do a lot of public speaking, it's really worth trying to find your own brand of humor that works. And if not, don't panic. It's not for everyone. There are plenty of other ways to connect.

YOUR TURN

16

YOUR VOICE

Halfway through a riveting talk on the power of memes, the philosopher Dan Dennett said this: "The secret of happiness is: find something more important than you are and dedicate your life to it."

Maybe you don't know what that is quite yet, and that's perfectly okay. But chances are, you care about something—the arts; the environment; equality for all, regardless of race, gender, or sexual orientation. Even though you might be too young to vote, you might still feel passionately about a political candidate. Or you might want to advocate for some group—homeless teens, for example, or immigrants. Your passion might be on either end of the political spectrum, but young voices are more essential than ever—and they are being heard.

We're strange creatures, we humans. On one hand, we just want to eat, drink, play, and acquire stuff. But on the other, we're moved to search out meaning, to make some contribution to the big human family.

Whatever it is you pursue, if you truly go after it, I predict two things: Yes, you'll find a meaningful form of happiness. And second, you'll discover something that matters far more than any advice you've read in this book—you'll discover *something worth saying.*

And then what? Well, then, of course, you must *share* it, using all the passion, skills, and determination you can muster. Share it in the way that ultimately only you will know how to do. Start a fire that will spread new wisdom far and wide.

Remember Malala Yousafzai? Her fire is education for girls and women around the world.

Emma González, David Hogg, Alex Wind, and other survivors of the shootings at Marjory Stoneman Douglas High School want to spread the fire of commonsense gun laws.

At just eight years old, Mari Copeny took up the cause of the water crisis in Flint, Michigan.

Jazz Jennings has become an advocate and symbol of hope for transgender youth struggling with issues of identity and acceptance.

And eleven-year-old Marley Dias started the #1000Black-GirlBooks campaign to donate books with black girls as main characters to other black girls, like her, who rarely found themselves on the pages of the books they read.

The list goes on and on and on. Young people lifting their voices, speaking out and acting on behalf of others, and changing the world along the way. But that change can feel more internal, as musician Anika Paulson explains in her TED Talk about music:

> I found myself through music. Music is everywhere, and it is in everything. And it changes and it builds and it

diminishes. But it's always there, supporting us, connecting us to each other and showing us the beauty of the universe.

So if you ever feel lost, stop and listen for your song.

I want a future in which young adults realize their potential to nudge the world in a positive direction. And that nudge always begins with an idea that, once spread, has the capacity to influence a limitless number of people, both now and in the future.

But what about those who would nudge the world in a bad direction? Can't public speaking be used for harm as well as good?

It can. However, I firmly believe that the growth of public speaking will mean a tilt to the positive—and young people will lead the way. Why? Because you're maturing during an unprecedented time of interconnectedness, when technology allows you to experience a much broader swath of the world than most adults did as teens. You're able to see into the lives of those different from yourselves, which helps create greater empathy and a feeling that, in so many ways, we're one.

When we're more closely connected—when people have full visibility of the world and one another—something different starts to happen. The speakers who will have the most influence will be those who succeed in tapping into those values and dreams that are most widely held.

I believe what we share is far more meaningful, more profound, than how we differ. We all hunger, yearn, suffer, laugh, weep, and love. We all bleed. We all dream. We are all capable of putting ourselves in others' shoes. It's possible for anyone with courage—of any age—to stand up and say something, to tap into this shared humanity and nurture it.

In the end, it's quite simple. We are physically connected to one another like never before. Which means that our ability to pass along our best ideas matters more than it ever has. The single greatest lesson I have learned from listening to TED Talks is this: *The future is not yet written. We are all, collectively, in the process of writing it.*

There's an open page—and an empty stage—waiting for you.

SOURCE NOTES

"At a primal level": Glenn Croston, "The Thing We Fear More Than Death," *Psychology Today*, November 29, 2012 (www.psychologytoday.com/us/blog/the-real-story-risk/201211/the-thing-we-fear-more-death; accessed December 15, 2018).

"Remember, never bend down": Luna Anderson, "What to Do If You See a Mountain Lion (Cougar)," *Hiker Track* (hikertrack.com/what-to-do-if-you-see-a-mountain-lion; accessed December 28, 2018).

"A perfectly normal human being": Patrick Allen, "How to Calm Your Nerves Before a Terrifying Speech," *Lifehacker* (lifehacker.com/how-to-calm-your-nerves-before-making-a-terrifying-spee-1677504967; accessed December 17, 2018).

"To bring anything into": Richard Bach, *The Bridge Across Forever* (New York: William Morrow, 1984).

INDEX